A Whiskey Might Not Fix Things, But It's Worth A Shot!

Whisk(e)y related:
Anecdotes, Humor, Jokes, Memes,
Quotes, Toasts & Trivia.

by
Paul Bissett

With thanks to all the smart, funny people that are quoted in this book. Without you our conversations would be boring.

Table of Contents

Chapter 1 – Anecdotes & Jokes 6

Chapter 2 – Hangovers 28

Chapter 3 – Memes 42

Chapter 4 – Quotes 79

Chapter 5 – Toasts 115

Chapter 6 – Facts, Stories & Trivia 128

Bibliography 195

Biography 200

Why this book

"Researching a subject on the internet is like drinking from a fire hose."

I, like many of you who have used the internet to do research for an upcoming event, have quickly realized that there is more information out there than you know what to do with. Invariably, you end up getting little bits of the necessary information from a variety of sources, which takes forever.

I have, with this book tried to distill (pun intended) down the information you might want, to prepare to talk in public at an event or just with your friends on the subject of drink in general, or whisk(e)y in particular.

I have been presenting whiskies, mainly scotch, but also whiskies from around the world, throughout California, Nevada, and Oregon for the last ten years. In preparing for these presentations I have acquired an in-depth knowledge of whisky; how it's made, its history, traditions, and whisky-related humor.

I have visited several distilleries in Scotland and spent a week at the Springbank Whisky School in Campbeltown, Scotland, working on all aspects of whisky making, from malting the barley to bottling and packaging the whisky.

I have tasted and written about whisky from every distillery currently producing whisky in Scotland, as well as whiskies from all the major (and some minor) regions worldwide.

I have written 5 other books on whisky;

"Scotland's Single Malt Whisky Distilleries"
Where they are, when they were founded, how to pronounce their names (and what those names mean). I have also included a review of a whisky from each distillery.

"Whisky Timeline" - Whisk(e)y distilleries around the world.

"Whisky Traveler America"
A guidebook to America's whiskey bars in every state.

"Whisky Traveler Great Britain"
A guidebook to whisk(e)y bars in England, Ireland, Northern Ireland, Scotland and Wales.

"Whisky Traveler"
A guidebook to the world's whisk(e)y bars listing over 1000 bars in 63 countries.

I have also given my thoughts on over 250 whiskies, in my newsletters that go out to 10 different countries.
I hope this book both informs and amuses my fellow whisk(e)y lovers out there.

Chapter 1

Anecdotes & Jokes

The professor stood in front of his class with a selection of items in front of him. When the lecture began, he took a very large glass, filled it up with large stones. When the glass was full, he asked the students:

"Is the glass full?"

Everyone agreed that it was.

The Professor took some very small stones, and gently poured them into the glass while he shakes it very carefully, causing the smaller stones to go in between the larger stones. When the glass again was filled up to the edge he asked once more:

"Is the glass full now?"

Everyone agreed that it was.

When the professor placed a bag with sand on the table the students laughed, of course the professor could add sand between the stones, and he filled it to the top.

"Now!" said the professor "Please imagine that this glass is your life!

The large stones are the meaningful things in your life, family, husband/wife, kids, your health etc., things that are important in your life.

The small stones are stuff not so important, like your job, house, car etc., the sand is everything else.

Please notice! If the glass is full of sand, there will be no room for small and large stones. It's the same in life, if you use your time and energy on small stuff there will be no room for important and meaningful stuff.
Always focus on which things are important for you, and your life will be great and happy.
Play with your kids, see the doctor, take care of your health, date your partner. There will always be time to work, clean up the house and do the smaller things!
Fill up your life with the things that really matter and are important. Check and arrange your large rocks and stones and keep in mind that the rest are only smaller stones and sand."

All the students can see the point!

The Professor now looks over the students and takes a glass of whisky, carefully he pours all the whisky between the sand, smaller and larger stones.

He looks up again and says:

"And the moral is! No matter what happens in your life there will always be room for whisky!"

Sir William Osler was lecturing one day to a group of medical students on the subject of intoxicating beverages.

"Is it true," asked one of his students, "that alcohol makes people able to do things better?"

"Not at all," replied the famous doctor. "It just makes them less ashamed of doing them badly.

****

A Scotsman buys an expensive bottle of whisky and puts it in his coat pocket. On his way home he falls and hits the ground hard. As he gets up, he feels a wet patch on his side.
"Please Lord" he prays "let it be blood.'

****

I was in a pub last Saturday night and had drank a few whiskies when I noticed two very large women at the bar.
They both had strong accents, so I asked,

"Hey, are you two ladies from Ireland?"

One of them replied saying, "It's WALES, you friggin' idiot!"

So, I immediately apologized and said,

"I'm sorry. Are you two whales from Ireland?"

That's pretty much the last thing I remember.

****

Whenever I give money to the homeless,
I get yelled at;

"They are just going to buy booze with that money."

All I can think is;

"Oh! Like I wasn't?

****

A woman is looking to re-enter the work force, now that her kids are all grown up. But before applying anywhere she goes to the doctors for a physical prior to starting a new job. When she returns, her husband, who is sat relaxing on the couch with a glass of whiskey, notices she's just bursting' with' pride and really happy.

So, he says; "What's all this about?"

She says, "I've just been to the doctors' and he said I've got the body of a twenty-year-old, and the heart of a 16-year-old".

To which her hubby fires back..."What about your 50-year-old ass?"

"Your name never came up." She replies!

****

An Irishman walks by a bar...it could happen.

****

I get dizzy after one drink. Usually the sixteenth.

****

I went fishing this morning but after a short time, I ran out of worms. Then I saw a cottonmouth with a frog in his mouth. Frogs are good bass bait. Knowing the snake couldn't bite me with the frog in his mouth I grabbed him right behind the head, took the frog, and put it in my bait bucket.
Now the dilemma was how to release the snake without getting bit. So, I grabbed my flask of Leiper's Fork Tennessee Whsikey and poured a little whiskey in its mouth. His eyes rolled back; he went limp. I released him into the lake without incident and carried on fishing using the frog.
A little later, I felt a nudge on my foot. It was that snake, with two more frogs.

****

A physician, observing Charles Banister, the great English actor, about to drink a glass of brandy, said: "Don't drink that filthy stuff; brandy is the worst enemy you have."
"I know that," responded Charles, "but you know we are commanded by scripture to love our enemies."

****

A horse walks into a bar and the bartender says "Hey".
The horse says "Sure".

In a convent in Tennessee, the 98-year-old Mother Superior lay dying. The nuns gathered around her bed, trying to make her last journey comfortable. They tried giving her warm milk to drink but she refused it. One of the nuns took the glass back to the kitchen.

Then, remembering a bottle of Leiper's Fork Tennessee whiskey that had been received as a gift the previous Christmas, she opened it and poured a generous amount into the warm milk.

Back at Mother Superior's bed, they held the glass to her lips. The frail nun drank a little, then a little more and before they knew it, she had finished the whole glass down to the last drop.

As her eyes brightened, the nuns thought it would be a good opportunity to have one last talk with their spiritual leader.

"Mother," the nuns asked earnestly, "Please give us some of your wisdom before you leave us."

She raised herself up in bed on one elbow, looked at them and said: "Don't sell that cow."

****

There were numerous rumors, that General Ulysses Grant drank too much,
and a delegation of Congressmen was appointed to find out the truth.

"Is it true," they asked him, "that you drink to excess?"

"To what? asked Grant.

"To excess," said the leader of the delegation.

"Well, why not?" said Grant.

"I just happen to have a bottle around, and if you don't mind taking it 'neat,' let's all have a pull at it.

Gentlemen, "To excess!"

****

A Scot rushed into a railway carriage in an excited state, shouting: "Whisky, quick - has anybody got a flask, a woman just fainted in the corridor."

An older gentleman produced a flask and handed it to the Scot.

The Scot unscrewed the cap and took a long drink, and handed it back to the owner, saying: "That's better.

It always upsets me to see a woman faint."

A doctor ordered the old vicar to take some hot whisky each day.

"But," objected the patient. I'm afraid my housekeeper would leave me if I did."
"She need not know, replied the doctor. Just tell her you want some shaving water."

Some weeks later the doctor called at the house to inquire for the vicar.

"He's gone quite mad sir, " quavered the housekeeper.
"The poor man is shaving himself morning noon and night."

****

Two guys are sitting at a bar.
One guy says to the other, "Do you know that lions have sex 10 or 15 times a night?".

The other guy says, "Damn, I just joined the Rotary Club."

****

A Scotsman is stranded on a desert island, all alone for ten years. One day a gorgeous woman wearing a wet suit and scuba gear swims up to the island. She approaches the Scotsman and says, "How long has it been since you had a cigarette?"

"Ten years!" he answers.

She reaches over, unzips the waterproof pocket on her left sleeve and pulls out a pack of fresh cigarettes.
He takes one, lights it, takes a long drag and says, "Man, oh man! Is that good!"
Then she asks, "How long has it been since you had a whisky?

He replies, "Ten years!"

She reaches over, unzips her waterproof pocket on the right sleeve, pulls out a bottle of single malt scotch and gives it to him.

He takes a long swallow and says, "Wow, that's fantastic!"

She then starts pulling down the long zipper that runs down the front of her wet suit and she says to him,

"And how long has it been since you played around?"

The Scotsman replies, "My God! Don't tell me you've a set of golf clubs in there!"

****

A professor of chemistry wanted to teach his 9th grade class a lesson about the evils of liquor, so he produced an experiment that involved a glass of water, a glass of whiskey, and two worms.

"Now, class. Observe closely the worms," said the professor putting a worm first into the water. The worm in the water writhed about, happy as a worm in water could be.

The second worm, he put into the whiskey. It writhed painfully, and quickly sank to the bottom, dead as a doornail.

"Now, what lesson can we derive from this experiment?" the professor asked.

Scott, who naturally sits in back, raised his hand and wisely, responded,

"Drink whiskey and you won't get worms."

****

A snail makes its way into a bar and tries to order a beer, but the bartender throws him out yelling "We don't serve snails in here!"
A few weeks later the same snail comes back into the bar and says to the bartender "What did you do that for?"

****

How a man can impress a woman:

Buy things for her
Care for her
Caress her
Comfort her
Compliment her
Cuddle her
Dine her
Hold her
Listen to her
Love her
Protect her
Stand by her
Tease her
Support her
and
Go to the ends of the earth for her.

How a woman can impress a man:

Show up naked
or
Bring Whisky

****

Returning from a trip to Europe, Mark Twain became annoyed as a customs official rummaged through his baggage.

"My good friend," the author exclaimed, "you don't have to mix up all my things. There are only clothes in there-nothing, but clothes."

But the suspicious fellow kept rooting about until he hit upon something hard. He pulled out a quart of the finest quality whisky.
You call this 'just clothes'?" cried the official.

"Sure thing," Twain replied calmly.
"That is my nightcap."

****

Doctor, to a patient's wife: Has your husband taken the medicine I prescribed? A pill before each meal and a small whisky after?"

Wife: "He's a few pills behind, but he's about a month ahead with the whisky."

****

Two nuns were shopping in a grocery store when they passed the beer and liquor section. The first nun asked the other if she would like a beer. The other nun answered that that would be good, but she was hesitant about purchasing beer in public. The first nun said she would handle it and picked up a six-pack and proceeded to the cashier.

The cashier had a surprised look on her face when she saw the beer. The first nun responded, "This is for washing our hair."

The cashier, without blinking an eye, reached under the counter and put a package of pretzel sticks in the bag with the beer saying,
"Here, don't forget the curlers."

****

The University of Nebraska says that elderly people that drink beer or wine at least four times a week have the highest bone density.
They need it - they're the ones falling down the most.

****

Three guys are drinking in a bar when a drunk comes in, staggers up to them, and points at the guy in the middle, shouting,

"Your mom's the best sex in town!" Everyone expects a fight, but the guy ignores him, so the drunk wanders off and bellies up to the bar at the far end. Ten minutes later, the drunk comes back, points at the same guy, and says, "I just did your mom, and it was sweeeeet!"

Again, the guy refuses to take the bait, and the drunk goes back to the far end of the bar.

Ten minutes later, he comes back and announces, "Your mom liked it!"

Finally, the guy interrupts. "Go home, Dad, you're drunk!

****

Ever since I was a child, I've always had a fear of someone under my bed at night. So, I went to a Psychiatrist and told him I've got problems. Every time I go to bed, I think there's somebody under it. I'm scared. I think I'm going crazy.

"Just put yourself in my hands for one year," said the psychiatrist. "Come talk to me three times a week and we should be able to get rid of those fears."

"How much do you charge?" "Eighty dollars per visit," replied the doctor.

"I'll sleep on it and if needed I will come back to you," I said.

Six months later the Psychiatrist met me on the street.

"Why didn't you come to see me about those fears you were having?" he asked.

"Well, eighty bucks a visit three times a week for a year is an awful lot of money! A bartender cured me for $10. I was so happy to have saved all that money that I went and bought me a new SUV."

"Is that so!" With a bit of an attitude he said, "and how, may I ask, did a bartender cure you?"

"He told me to cut the legs off the bed – ain't nobody under there now!"

****

A man had been drinking at the bar for hours when he mentioned something about his girlfriend being out in the car.

The bartender, concerned because it was so cold, went to check on her. When he looked inside the car, he saw the drunk's buddy, Pete, and his girlfriend going at it in the backseat.

The bartender shook his head and walked back inside. He told the drunk that he thought it might be a good idea to check on his girlfriend.

The drunk staggered outside to the car, saw Pete and his girlfriend entwined, then walked back into the bar laughing.

"What's so funny?" the bartender asked.

"That damned Pete!" the drunk chortled, "He's so drunk, he thinks he's me!"

****

A man walks into a bar and orders a 12-year-old scotch. The bartender, believing that the customer will not be able to tell the difference, pours him a shot of the cheap 3-year-old house scotch that has been poured into an empty bottle of the good stuff. The man takes a sip and spits the scotch out on the bar and reams the bartender.
"This is the cheapest 3-year-old scotch you can buy. I'm not paying for it. Now, give me a good 12-year-old scotch."
The bartender, now feeling a bit of a challenge, pours him a scotch of much better quality, 6-year-old scotch. The man takes a sip and spits it out on the bar.
"This is only 6-year-old scotch. I won't pay for this, and I insist on a good, 12-year-old scotch. The bartender finally relents and serves the man his best quality, 12-year-old scotch. The man sips the drink and says, "Now that's more like it."

An old drunk from the end of the bar, who has witnessed the entire episode, walks down to the finicky scotch drinker and sets a glass down in front of him and asks, "What do you think of this?"

The scotch expert takes a sip, and in disgust, violently spits out the liquid yelling "THIS TASTES LIKE PISS."

To which the old drunk replies, "That's right, now guess how old I am."

****

Two men were sitting at the bar, each having the latest in a long series of drams, when they struck up a conversation. "Where are you from?" asked the first.

"Mull," replied the second.

"Well, well, I'm a Tobermory man myself."

"Me too, what street in Tobermory?"

At that point the landlord came in to ask the barman how things were going.

"Ach fine," he replied "except the Maclean twins are drunk again."

****

What's the difference between a battery and a whisky?
A battery has a negative side.

****

The bartender asks the guy sitting at the bar, "What'll you have?" The guy answers, "A scotch, please."

The bartender hands him the drink and says, "That'll be ten dollars." To which the guy replies,

"What are you talking about? I don't owe you anything for this."

A lawyer, sitting nearby and overhearing the conversation, then says to the bartender, "You know, he's got you there. In the original offer, which constitutes a binding contract upon acceptance, there was no stipulation of remuneration."

The bartender was not impressed, but says to the guy, "Okay, you beat me for a drink. But don't ever let me catch you in here again."

The next day, the same guy walks into the bar. The Bartender says, "What the heck are you doing in here? I can't believe you've got the audacity to come back!"
The guy says, "What are you talking about? I've never been in this place in my life!"

The bartender replies, "I'm very sorry, but this is uncanny. You must have a double."

To which the guy replies, "Thank you. Make it a scotch."

****

A recent study conducted by Glasgow University found that the average Scotsman walks about 900 miles a year.
Another study by the Scottish Medical association found that Scotsmen drink on average, 22 gallons of alcohol a year.
This means, on average, Scotsmen get about 41 miles to the gallon.

****

A real woman is a man's best friend. She will never stand him up and never let him down. She will reassure him when he feels insecure and comfort him after a bad day.
She will inspire him to do things, he never thought he could do; To live without fear and forget regret. She will enable him to express his deepest emotions and give in to his most intimate desires.
She will make sure he always feels as though he is the most handsome man in the room and will enable him to be the most confident, sexy, seductive and invincible.....NO WAIT!
Sorry..
I'm thinking of whisky.
It's whisky that does all that stuff.....never mind.

****

"McDougall's dead. He fell into a vat of whisky."

"What a shame, was it a quick death?'

"I don't think so, he came out twice to go to the bathroom."

****

Chapter 2

Hangovers

"I'll never drink again."

After twenty-three years travelling the world with the British Royal Navy and overindulging in many of the ports we stopped in, I believe that I know what a bad hangover feels like.
In those visits to over forty countries, both in the Navy and afterwards as an older, and I hope wiser civilian I came across some strange hangover cures and learned what works best for me.
Hopefully in this chapter, I can help you find out what is best for you.

Depending on what and how much you drank, you might have:

- Decreased ability to concentrate
- Dizziness
- Fatigue and weakness
- Headaches and muscle aches
- Increased sensitivity to light and sound
- Mood disturbances, such as depression, anxiety and irritability

- Nausea, vomiting and/or stomach pain
- Poor or decreased sleep
- Rapid heartbeat
- Shakiness
- Thirst

At the very least you are going to feel like C&@P!!

What works for me? When I was a newly minted drinker (18 in the UK), I would wake up feeling terrible and just tough it out.
As I got older and more experienced, I would set my alarm for about an hour before I had to get up and take some pain killers with a drink of water, then go back to sleep, which initially, still had some pain involved.
I was in my forties when my American wife told me to take a couple of pain killers and a drink of water before I went to sleep, which works perfectly, no headache, just maybe a little thirsty, but overall not too bad.
DAMN, why didn't I think of that, about a thousand hangovers previously.

Hangover cures?

In Australia if you wake up with a hangover get yourself some "Berocca" and drop a couple of tablets into a glass of cold water.
You will get a drink that contains a high level of vitamins B, C. plus added magnesium, calcium and zinc, which helps your body to rehydrate.

In Bangladesh drink coconut water to relieve your hangover blues, this is nature's energy drink with lots of sodium and Potassium.

In Canada they swear by "Poutine" A combination of French fries and cheese curds topped with beef gravy, a greasy perfection, which tastes delicious. Eaten after your drinking is done and before you head home to bed.

In China "Congee" for breakfast, is how it's done, this rice porridge doesn't have a whole lot of nutritional value, but it will leave you feeling full and hydrated.

In Croatia they eat "Burek" a meat and cheese pastry. The dough soaks up the alcohol, while the meat and cheese slow down the alcohol absorption into your body.

In France it's "Cassoulet" (bean and meat casserole) that they turn to when hung-over. This dish is high in carbs and proteins for faster restoration of your body, but you better prepare in advance, to make it properly takes three days.

In Germany "pickled Herring" is what revives the locals. This fish dish helps restore the calories, protein, fat, salt and electrolytes you need to recover.

In Haiti there is a voodoo cure for hangovers, which entails sticking 13 pins into the cork from the bottle you drank from.

In Iceland "Sheep's Head" served in a terrine or jelly, has everything your body needs to help it recover.

In India if you have overindulged at some of the best whisky bars in the world, get yourself some herbal tea, these have lots of antioxidants, which help your liver process the toxins you've ingested.
If you are feeling nauseous have them add some ginger to settle your stomach.

In Italy they just stick to their morning espresso to cure their hangovers.

In Japan "Umiboshi" is the dish that sets the locals back on track, this is a dish of pickled plums or apricots (Both sweet and sour), which can help prevent nausea.

In Mexico a tripe-based soup called "Menudo" with cilantro, hominy, red chilies, and chunks of beef, is a popular hangover cure.

In Mongolia a creamy meat soup called "Bantan" is good for what ails you.

In Peru Ceviche (fish and/or seafood, cooked in citrus juice) is the dish of choice to revive you after a good night out with lots of vitamin B and C.

In Poland they drink sour pickle juice to cure their hangovers.

In Romania as in Mexico their go to for a hangover is a tripe soup, this time with root vegetable, garlic and cream.

In South Africa an omelet made from an ostrich egg (approx., 3-pounds), the equivalent of two dozen chicken eggs is the cure for locals.
I assume this is a dish for more than one person.

In the Netherlands they just go down the "Hair of the dog" route and recommend a couple of cold beers to recover from a hangover.

In the Philippines "Balut" is the cure of choice, these are fertilized duck eggs. Crack the shell and you'll find a fully formed embryo with beak and feathers. Happy crunching!

In Scotland the full cooked Scottish breakfast or a glass of "IRN BRU" or possibly both. "IRN BRU" is a soft drink (soda), that is so popular, that it is known as their other national drink.

In Spain the locals swear by "Pinch de Tortilla" bites sized potato omelet gives your hangover the carbohydrates and protein it craves.

In the UK the perceived wisdom is a full English/Irish/Scottish breakfast (not sure if the Welsh agree), I have heard the Welsh recommend laver bread (made from seaweed).
The breakfast consists of fried sausage, bacon, eggs, tomato, bread, black pudding (and Haggis in Scotland), fried mushrooms and beans (not usually fried).
Eggs are common hangover aids, rich in protein, minerals and fats, which help to break down the acetaldehyde in the alcohol you drank the previous

evening and the grease has cholesterol which your liver uses as a fuel.
So, if you have the urge to eat a big fried breakfast and you can keep it down, it will probably make you feel better.

One cure from the middle ages involves slicing up an eel and spreading bitter almonds over it, before eating.

Hair of the Dog

The "hair of the dog" doctrine is supposedly a myth; I would disagree with the medical profession on that one.
They tell us that we are just delaying the inevitable, by drinking more alcohol, putting off the hangover until later.
If you have a "Hair of the dog" it's just a hair not the whole dog, like you had the night before.
Done correctly, such as with a bloody Mary (or two), you ease your way back to sobriety, while removing the pain.
I believe that it has worked for me, but the choice is yours, it's your hangover.
Much better than this alternative, in Mongolia, their "Mongolian Mary," is a pickled sheep eye in tomato juice.

Other dog hairs include;

The American - "Prairie Oyster" an egg yolk, Worcestershire sauce, Tabasco sauce, salt and pepper, thrown back and swallowed in one gulp.

The Danish - "Reparationsbajer" In Denmark, people drink "Repair beer," because it makes them feel better.

The Mexican - "Micheladas" which is lime juice, peppers and spices mixed with beer, served in a salt-rimmed glass.

The Namibian - "Buffalo milk," comprising dark rum, spiced rum, cream liqueur and whole cream.

The Russian - "Kvas" a mildly alcoholic drink made with rye bread soaked in sugar and yeast.

Hangover Cure Products - Better living through chemistry

Apart from the obvious painkillers you can buy, you might like to try some of these hangover cure products. I can't personally recommend any of them as I haven't tried any.

Blowfish
The fizzy tabs include max strength pain relievers and extra caffeine to get you back on your feet. They guarantee to make you feel better in about 15 minutes. They also offer a money back guarantee if it fails.

Drinkade
Offered in either Prevention or Boost. Prevention (limeade flavor) drink before your night out.
Boost (Berry flavor) caffeine and Vitamin B-12, for the morning after.

Morning Recovery Drink
Morning Recovery Drink can also be taken the night before as a nightcap, which should mean you have no hangover in the morning.

Resqwater
Resqwater has B vitamins, cane sugar, electrolytes, milk thistle, prickly pear and water to help your body recover.

How you got your hangover
An article in "the Atlantic" magazine traced the history of the many words and phrases that English-speaking folks around the world have developed to express the simple fact that someone has had too many drinks.
Enjoy this list of the many, ways to express the simple fact that someone had one too many.
Before we begin, we should address the word *drunk* itself. We can trace it back to the Middle English "fordrunken." So, the word "drunk" showed up on the scene in the 1500s.

Here are some more, some old some relatively new;

Blotto - As in, soaks up alcohol like blotting paper soaks up ink

Brown bottle flu - kind of obvious where this one comes from

Bumpsy - Inspired by the "staggering gait" of drunks bumping into things

Crapulence - Ye olde word from the 16th century

Groggy - Having had too much grog, the sailor's drink of rum and water

High - Before the Brits started using marijuana, it was used for being drunk.

Honkers - Among its many possible roots is the slang verb "honk," or vomit. Also, the nickname for Hong Kong in the British Navy, where sailors drink a lot.

Katzenjammer - Nineteenth-century American slang, from the German for 'wailing cats.

Lushy - From the slang "lush," meaning any kind of beer or liquor

Plonked - From "plonk," from the term used for cheap wine

Poggled - Has its origins in the Hindi word pagal, for "madman"

Tippled - For tippler, the name for a tavern-keeper

Wasted - Hippy invention from the 1960's

What about the phrase "three sheets to the wind?" This is a nautical reference to a three-cornered sail held in place by ropes. These ropes were called "sheets," and were used to control a ships course. When the sheets came loose, the ship would zig-zag around the sea like a drunken sailor.

If you've ever experienced a hangover, the Polish phrase for such an event will resonate: a "howling of kittens."

What follows are approximate translations of phrases used to refer to a hangover around the world.

China: "Drunk Overnight"

Denmark: "Carpenters in the forehead."

Egypt: "Still Drunk"

El Salvador: "Wake up 'made of rubber."

France: "Wake up 'with a wooden mouth' or a 'hair ache (not used as much today)."

Germany & The Netherlands: "Have a 'tomcat (yowling in your head)."

Japan: "Two Days Drunk"

Sweden: "Smacked from Behind"

Hangover thoughts

"A hangover is just your body telling you that you are an idiot."

****

"A hangover is nature's way of grounding you as an adult."

****

"A real hangover is nothing to try out family remedies on.
The only cure for a real hangover is death."

Robert Benchley

****

Dejabrew

(n) Slowly remembering things, you did while drunk.

****

"Grease is the only cure for a hangover."

Cameron Diaz

****

"For a bad hangover, take the juice of a bottle of whisky."

****

Hangover:

Something to occupy a head that wasn't used the night before.

****

"I feel sorry for people who don't drink. When they wake up in the morning, that's as good as they're going to feel all day."

Dean Martin

****

People who help you find what you're looking for in a liquor store.
Should be called "Spirit guides."

****

Please God cure my hangover and I promise
I will never drink again,
also please forgive me in advance for lying about never drinking again.

****

"The light did him harm, but not as much as looking at things did.
He resolved, having done it once, never to move his eyeballs again."

Kingsley Amis

****

We can put a man on the moon, but we still haven't found a way to prevent a hangover.

Priorities people come on!

****

"What in the world is a hangover cure?"

Brian Wilson

****

"When I have supped too heavily of an evening, I drink in the morning a large number of cups of coffee, and that as hot as I can drink it, so that the sweat breaks out on me, and if by so doing I can't restore my body, a whole apothecary's shop couldn't do much, and that is the only thing I have done for years when I have felt a fever."

Antonie van Leeuwenhoek

Chapter 3

Memes

A banana is 105 calories.
A shot of whiskey is 80 calories.
Choose wisely.

****

A friend walks in with whisky,
when everyone else walks out.

****

A person with a basement full of whiskey.......Alcoholic

A person with a basement full of wine........Classy

****

A popular meme on Facebook states:

In the old west a .45 cartridge for a six-gun cost 12 cents, so did a glass of whiskey. If a cowhand was low on cash, he would often give the bartender a cartridge in exchange for a drink. This became known as a "shot" of whiskey.

"Unfortunately, there is no evidence to support this story,
but I still like the idea of it."

****

A whisky bottle contains more philosophy, than all the books in the world.

****

After five drinks, they play the Star-Spangled Banner to see who can still stand up.

****

After my fourth whiskey, I swear I heard it whisper; Now is the time to tell people what you really think."

****

Age gets better with whiskey.

****

Alcohol:

A liquid; good for preserving almost everything, except secrets.

****

Alcohol and calculus don't mix, so don't drink and derive

****

Alcohol is the liquid version of Photoshop.

****

Alcohol and Fats:

It's a relief to know the truth after all those conflicting medical studies;

The Japanese eat very little fat and suffer fewer heart attacks than the British or Americans.

The French eat a lot of fat and suffer fewer heart attacks than the British or Americans.

The Italians drink excessive amounts of red wines and suffer fewer heart attacks than the British or Americans.

The Germans drink a lot of beer and eat lots of sausages and fats and suffer fewer heart attacks than the British or Americans.

Conclusion:

Eat and drink what you like. Speaking English is apparently what kills you.

****

Alcoholic!

I prefer the term drinking enthusiast.

****

A whisky might change things.

****

Bartender:

A guy in a white jacket who brings you into contact with the spirit world.

****

Beauty is in the eye of the beer holder.

****

Before coffee became popular, beer was often served for breakfast in the United States.

****

Booze:

Better than therapy.

****

Civil war soldiers getting a leg sawn off, were never given a Vodka and Cranberry.
Just order a whiskey already.

****

Courage is a vitamin best swallowed with whiskey

****

Dance and song:

Two things that become very easy after a few drinks.

****

Dear alcohol, we had a deal where you would make me funnier, smarter, and a better dancer...
I saw the video; we need to talk.

****

Did you know that before the invention of the crowbar? crows had to do their drinking at home.

****

Don't drink and drive, you might spill your drink.

****

Drink whisky and ignore stuff.

****

Drinking:

An act that doesn't drown your sorrows- only irrigates them.

****

Drinking rum before 10am makes you a pirate, not a drunk.

****

Drunk is when you feel sophisticated but can't pronounce it.

****

Drunkard:

A fellow who is always going to quit after the next one, instead of the last one.

****

Education is important, but whisky is importanter.

****

Everyone has a hidden talent, they don't know about, until the whiskey is poured.

****

Friend: So, what's your favorite drink?

Me: The next one.

****

Friends like mine are hard to find......
there are so many pubs and they could be in any of them.

****

Friendship is like whisky, the older the better.

****

Forecast for tonight:

Alcohol, low standards and poor decisions.

****

God invented whiskey,
so, the Irish would never take over the world.

****

I was trying to write a drinking song,
but couldn't get past the first few bars.

****

I am not drunk!
I am by nature a loud obnoxious,
clumsy person with a speech impediment.

****

I don't drink alcohol, I drink spirits.
So, I'm not an alcoholic, I'm spiritual.

****

I don't drink anything stronger than pop.
And pop will drink anything.

****

I don't even believe myself,
when I say I'm only going to have one drink?

****

I don't pretend to be anything I'm not...
Except for sober, I've pretended to be sober a few times.

****

I drank so much scotch last night,
I woke up with a Scottish accent.

****

I drink on Sundays to cope with the realization,
that I am almost out of time to drink.

****

I'd rather be someone's shot of whisky, than
everybody's cup of tea.

****

I go to work so I can afford the amount of alcohol
required to continue to go to work.

****

I like to have at least five practice beers,
before I have my actual beer.

****

I only drink whisky on days ending in 'Y'.

****

I only drink whisky on two occasions, when it's my birthday
and when it's not my birthday.

****

If life was easy, we wouldn't need alcohol.

****

If the question is whisky related,
the answer is yes.

****

If whisky can't fix it,
you're not using enough whisky.

****

If you don't drink,
how will your friends know you love them at 2am?

****

If you have to ask if it's too early to drink whisky.
You're an amateur and we can't be friends.

****

If you see your glass as half empty,
pour it into a smaller glass and stop bitching.

****

I have reached the age where falling asleep on the couch has nothing to do with coming home drunk.

****

I like long romantic walks……to the whisky bar.

****

I'll tell you what's wrong with society,
no-one drinks from the skulls of their enemies
anymore.

****

I need a huge glass of scotch.

****

I really love water, especially if it's frozen
and surrounded with whiskey.

****

I think my car needs an alignment,
it always pulls towards the liquor store.

****

I think my guardian angel drinks!

****

I told myself I should stop drinking......
But I'm not about to listen to some drunk who talks to himself.

****

I used to think that drinking was bad for me,
so, I gave up thinking.

****

I went to the liquor store Friday afternoon on my bicycle, bought a bottle of scotch and put it in the bicycle basket.
As I was about to leave, I thought to myself that if I fell off, the bottle would break. So, I drank all the scotch before I cycled home.
It turned out to be a very good decision, because I fell off seven times on my way home.

****

If you apply a little whisky to that bad mood,
it takes the sting right out.

****

If you walk a mile in my shoes,
you'll just end up in a bar

****

I'm in a good place right now.
Not emotionally,
I'm at the liquor store.

****

I'm kinda glad dinosaurs are extinct,
because I'm pretty sure that I would try to ride one
after a few drinks.

****

I'm not an alcoholic,
I just have a lot of reasons to celebrate.

****

I'm a Marathon runner......Just kidding, I'm a whiskey
drinker.

****

I'm watching my drinking.
I only visit bars that have mirrors.

****

In an effort to conserve water....
I've stopped having it in my whisky.
We've all got to do our bit for the planet.

****

It's not really drinking alone...
If the dog is home.

****

It's time to impress everyone with your dance moves.
Sincerely....your fifth whiskey.

****

I've been on the whisky diet...
I've lost three days already.

****

"I've often been asked, what do you old folks do now that you're retired?"

"Well I'm......fortunate to have a chemical engineering, background and one of the things I enjoy most is converting beer, wine and whisky into urine.
I do it every day and I really enjoy it."

****

I wish there was a morning-after pill,
for when I drunkenly post something on Facebook.

****

"Just because you can't sing,
doesn't mean that you shouldn't."

Alcohol

****

Keep your friends close,
but your whisky closer.

****

Laughter may be the best medicine,
but a bottle of whisky makes a pretty good band-aid.

****

Lewis and Clark didn't load the canoe with Mojitos.
Just order a whiskey already.

****

Life is not a fairytale, if you lose your shoe at midnight.
You might want to ease back on the whisky.

****

Looks like you have a lot on your mind.
Do you want to drink about it?

****

May the good lord preserve us
from the disease that whisky cannot cure.

****

My doctor told me to drink more water,
so, I added an ice cube to my whiskey.

****

My doctor told me to watch my drinking,
so, I'm off to find a bar with a mirror

****

Never cry over spilt milk.
It could have been whisky

****

Never send a beer to do a whiskies job.

****

Of course, size matters.
No-one wants a small cocktail.

****

One day I will solve all my problems with maturity.
But today, it will be with alcohol.

****

People tell me I should drink less whisky,
but I can't find that brand anywhere.

****

People who say I'm hard to shop for,
obviously don't know where to buy whisky.

****

People who wonder whether the glass is half empty
or half full miss the point.
The glass is refillable.

****

Pour yourself a whisky and deal with it.

****

Procrastadrinking:

The art of drinking instead of doing something else you should be doing.

****

Ran out of creamer and milk for my coffee this morning, luckily, I still had whisky.

****

Right now, I'd rather be drinking whisky.

****

Saying I have a drinking problem is like saying Bruce Lee had a Kung Fu problem.
It's not a problem if you're the best at it.

****

Scotch the breakfast of champions:

Gaelic words for an early morning dram;

Sgailc-nide - A whisky while still lying down in bed.

Friochd-uilinn - A whisky when first propped up in bed.

Deoch chasruigte - A whisky while still Barefoot.

Deoch Bhleth - A whisky while your oatmeal is being prepared.

Skalk - Spirits taken before breakfast.

****

Scotch; The next best thing to being there.

****

Seen on a board outside a pub:

We have beer as cold as your ex-girlfriend's heart.

****

She was only a whisky maker, but he loved her still.

****

Sometimes I drink a glass of water...
just to surprise my liver.

****

Sometimes I think to myself:

Do I want a whiskey?
And then I remember, there's a super volcano under Yellowstone that is 400,000 years overdue and when it erupts, could potentially cover most of North America in ash and create a volcanic winter
that would kill half of the world's population and I'm like,
"HELL, YES I WANT A WHISKEY."

****

Sometimes my terrible life decisions,
look like fantastic drinking opportunities.

****

Stop posting your problems on Facebook.
Go to a bar like everyone else.

****

Studies show that carrots improve your vision.
Whisky doubles it!

****

Sure, I'll go on a run with you.
But only if it's to the liquor store.
And we drive there.

****

That Burn you feel when you drink whisky.
That's your soul healing.

****

Technically:

According to Chemistry, Whisky is a solution.

****

The consumption of alcohol may create the illusion that you are tougher, smarter and better looking than most people.

****

"The men rode into the saloon," is never followed by and "ordered a Merlot."
Just order a whiskey already.

****

The only thing I learned from Geography is Long Island has the best iced tea.

****

There are better things in the world than alcohol, but alcohol sort of compensates for not getting them.

****

They say that alcohol kills slowly.........So what? Who's in a hurry.

****

They say that money can't buy happiness,
but I have a receipt from the liquor store telling a whole different story.

****

They should put whisky in bigger bottles,
so, there is enough for two people.

****

Think positively:

While the glass may be half empty, the pub is still open.

****

Thirty days sober folks!

Not consecutively,
but here and there over the last twenty years.

****

This whiskey tastes like I'm about to tell you,
how I really feel.

****

To do list:

Open bottle, pour whisky, drink whisky, repeat.

****

Today I found out the average person drinks four beers a week.
Today I also found out that I am above average.

****

Today's rain is tomorrow's whisky.

****

To relieve stress, I do yoga...
Just kidding!
I drink whiskey in my yoga pants.

****

Top 10 rules of Boozing:

1. It's ok to drink alone

2. Vodka can be mixed with anything, including more vodka.

3. In wine there is wisdom; in beer there is strength, but whisky is the water of life.

4. Drunken words are sober thoughts; listen carefully.

5. If you do something really stupid, never blame it on the booze or on being drunk.

6. If he/she is still ugly after seven drinks, give up.

7. Beer is food, wine accompanies food, cocktails demand food.

8. An open bar is a dangerous game, respect it.

9. Never turn down a free drink or complain about its quality or brand.

10. Always stick around for one more drink, that's when things happen.

Tip your bartender – if it wasn't for us you would still be sober.

****

Today's forecast.......100% chance of whisky.

****

To me:

Drink responsibly means, don't spill it.

****

Unless your kid's fundraiser is selling whiskey, I'm not really interested.

****

WARNING!

Alcohol consumption will make you believe you're whispering.
I assure you, you're not.

****

WARNING!

Drinking alcoholic beverages before pregnancy, can cause pregnancy

****

WARNING:

When you drink vodka over ice it can give you kidney failure.

When you drink rum over ice it can give you liver failure.

When you drink whisky over ice it can give you heart failure.

When you drink gin over ice it can give you brain problems.

Apparently, ice is really bad for you!

****

"What soberness conceals.
Drunkenness reveals."

****

What whiskey and butter will not cure?
there is no cure for.

Irish proverb

****

When life gives you lemons, sell them to buy whisky.

****

What else can make us happy
If women and drink cannot do it?

****

Whenever I have a panic attack, I put a brown paper bag
over my mouth...
and drink all the Bourbon inside.
It seems to help.

****

Whenever someone asks me if I want water in my scotch?
I tell them I'm thirsty, not dirty

****

Whisky!

Because no great story started with someone drinking water.

****

Whisky!

Because you don't win friends with salad.

****

Whisky is like a kiss, you'll enjoy it more,
if you share it with someone you like.

****

Whisky is my Spirit animal.

****

Whisky is sunlight held together by water.

****

Whisky is what beer wants to be when it grows up.

****

Whisky!
Making people less boring since roughly the 15th century.

****

Whisky may not solve your problems,
but neither does milk.

****

Whiskey may shorten your life,
but you'll see twice as much in half the time.

****

Whiskey Wednesday, it's like Taco Tuesday,
but for badasses.

****

Whisky taster;
Will work for free!

****

Wife: I'm heading to the store; do you want anything?

Husband: I want a sense of meaning and purpose in my life I seek fulfillment and completeness to my soul. I want to connect to God and discover the spiritual side to me...

Wife: Be specific - Black label or Chivas?

****

With my lineage,
I'm surprised I don't pour whisky on my cornflakes.

****

Whoever said that laughter was the best medicine,
had clearly never tasted whisky.

****

"You can kick his ass."

Whisky

****

You can't buy happiness,
but you can buy whisky and that's pretty close.

****

You're making too many sober decisions.

****

Chapter Four

Quotes

"A drink a day keeps the shrink away."

Edward Abbey

****

"A party without alcohol is just a meeting."

A. Wiseman

****

"A sea of whiskey couldn't intoxicate me as much as a drop of you."

J.S. Parker

****

"Alcohol gives you infinite patience for stupidity."

Sammy Davis, Jr.

****

"Alcohol is a liquid that can put the wreck into recreation."

Anonymous

****

"Alcohol is necessary for a man so that he can have a good opinion of himself, undisturbed by the facts."

Finley Peter Dunne

****

"Alcohol may be man's worst enemy, but the bible says love your enemy."

Frank Sinatra

****

"Alcohol is the anesthesia by which we endure the operation of life."

George Bernard Shaw

****

"Always carry a large flagon of whisky in case of snakebite and furthermore always carry a small snake."

W. C. Fields

****

"Always do sober what you said you'd do drunk. That will teach you to keep your mouth shut."

Ernest Hemingway

****

"Any man that eats dessert is not drinking enough."

Ernest Hemmingway

****

"As they say around the Texas Legislature, if you can't drink their whiskey, screw their women, take their money, and vote against 'em anyway, you don't belong in office."

Molly Ivins

****

"Be wary of strong drink.
It can make you shoot at tax collectors... and miss."

Robert A. Heinlein

****

"By the time a bartender knows what drink a man will have before he orders, there is little else about him worth knowing."

Don Marquis

****

"Do you understand about water in the West? Whiskey's for drinking; water's for fightin' over."

Paul Gosar

****

"Drink because you are happy, but never because you are miserable."

G. K. Chesterton

****

"Drink! for you know not whence you came nor why: drink! for you know not why you go, nor where."

Omar Khayyam

****

"Drink is the only opponent I have been unable to beat."

George Best

****

"Drink moderately, for drunkenness neither keeps a secret, nor observes a promise."

Miguel de Cervantes

****

"Drinking makes such fools of people, and people are such fools to begin with that it's compounding a felony."

Robert Benchley

****

"Drown in a cold vat of whiskey? Death, where is thy sting?"

W. C. Fields

****

"Freedom and whisky gang the gither."

Robert Burns

****

"Giving money and power to government is like giving whiskey and car keys to teenage boys."

P. J. O'Rourke

****

"Happiness is having a rare steak, a bottle of whiskey, and a dog to eat the rare steak."

Johnny Carson

****

"Here lies one who might be trusted with untold gold, but not with unmeasured whisky."

Sir Walter Scott's epitaph for his favorite servant, Tom Purdie

****

"Here's to alcohol: the cause of, and answer to, all of life's problems."

Matt Groening

****

"Humanity I love you because when you're hard up, you pawn your intelligence to buy a drink."

E. E. Cummings

****

"I am a drinker, with a writing problem."

Brendan Behan

****

"I am more afraid of alcohol than of all the bullets of the enemy."

Stonewall Jackson

****

"I am not a heavy drinker.
I can sometimes go for hours without touching a drop."

Noel Coward

****

"I drink my whiskey neat and live my life messy."

Matt Baker

****

"I know I'm drinking myself to a slow death, but then I'm in no hurry."

Robert Benchley

****

"If I cannot drink Bourbon and smoke cigars in Heaven, then I shall not go."

Mark Twain

****

"If I had all the money I'd spent on drink,
I'd spend it on drink."

Vivian Stanshall

****

"If you are young and you drink a great deal it will spoil your health, slow your mind, make you fat - in other words, turn you into an adult."

P. J. O'Rourke

****

"If you drink don't drive. Don't even putt."

Dean Martin

****

"If you resolve to give up smoking, drinking and sex, you don't actually live longer; it just seems longer."

Clement Freud

****

"I distrust camels, and anyone else who can go a week without a drink."

Joe E. Lewis

****

"I don't drink any more than the man next to me, and the man next to me is Dean Martin."

Joe E. Lewis

****

"I drink no more than a sponge."

Francois Rabelais

****

"I drink therefore I am."

W. C. Fields

****

"I drink to forget I drink."

Joe E. Lewis

****

"I drink to make other people interesting."

George Jean Nathan

****

"I drink too much.
The last time I gave a urine sample it had an olive in it."

Rodney Dangerfield

****

"I envy people who drink - at least they know what to blame everything on."

Oscar Levant

****

I have a reputation for drinking a lot. Indeed, I drink quite much.
However, I give it up when I wish to do so.
I never, ever drink while on duty.
The drinking is only for my pleasure.
I do not remember neglecting my duties because of drinking even once."

Mustafa Kemal Ataturk

****

"I have never in my life seen a Kentuckian who didn't have a gun, a pack of cards, and a jug of whiskey."

Andrew Jackson

****

"I have a punishing workout regimen.
Every day I do 3 minutes on a treadmill, then I lie down, drink a glass of vodka and smoke a cigarette."

Anthony Hopkins

****

"I have taken more out of alcohol, than alcohol has taken out of me."

Winston Churchill

****

"I like my whisky old and my women young."

Errol Flynn

****

"I like to drink to suit my location."

Tom Jones

****

"I like whiskey.
I always did, and that is why I never drink it."

Robert E. Lee

****

"I love a scotch that's old enough to order its own scotch."

Robin Sherbatsky

****

"I love to sing, and I love to drink scotch.
Most people would rather hear me drink scotch."

George Burns

****

"I love whiskey and haggis. I can't get enough of either."

Kevin McKidd

****

"I'll never feel comfortable taking a strong drink,
and I'll never feel easy smoking a cigarette.
I just don't think those things are right for me."

Elvis Presley

****

"I'm a beer man. I tried to drink whiskey and Scotch, but I don't get it.
It smells like a girl who didn't shower and just splashed a lot of perfume on."

Mads Mikkelsen

****

"I'm a simple man.
All I want is enough sleep for two normal men, enough whiskey for three, and enough women for four."

Joel Rosenberg

****

"I may be drunk, Madam, but in the morning I will be sober, and you will still be ugly."

Winston Churchill

****

"I must have a drink of breakfast."

W.C. Fields

****

"I never diet. I smoke. I drink now and then.
I never work out."

Naomi Campbell

****

"I never trust a fighting man who doesn't smoke or drink."

Admiral William "Bull" Halsey

****

"I never turned to drink. It seemed to turn to me."

Brendan Behan

****

"I should never have switched from scotch to martinis."

Humphrey Bogart's last words

****

"I try not to drink too much because when I'm drunk, I bite."

Bette Midler

****

"I was in London.
It's a long way to go for a very long party,
sitting there for six hours not having a cigarette or a drink.
It's a waste of time."

Albert Finney

****

"I was in love with a beautiful blonde once.
She drove me to drink.
That's the one thing I'm indebted to her for."

W. C. Fields

****

"I wish to live to 150-years-old,
but the day I die,
I wish it to be with a cigarette in one hand a whiskey
in the other."

Ava Gardner

****

"In 1969, I gave up women and alcohol - it was the worst 20 minutes of my life."

George Best

****

"Is the glass half full or half empty, it depends on whether your pouring or drinking."

Bill Cosby

****

"It is not true that drink changes a man's character. It may reveal it more clearly."

John Osborne

****

"It takes only one drink to get me drunk. The trouble is, I can't remember if it's the thirteenth or the fourteenth."

George Burns

****

"It was my Uncle George who discovered that alcohol was a food well in advance of modern medical thought."

P. G. Wodehouse

****

"I think a man ought to get drunk at least twice a year just on principle, so he won't get snotty about it."

Raymond Chandler

****

"I write and walk and swim and drink."

John le Carre

****

"Let him who sins when drunk, be punished when sober."

Legal maxim

****

"If a body could just find oot the exac' proper proportion and quantity that ought to be drunk every day, and keep to that, I verily trow that he might leev forever, without dyin' at a', and that doctors and kirkyards would go out of fashion."

The Ettrick Sheppard

****

"Love makes the world go round. Whisky makes it go round twice as fast."

Compton Mackenzie

****

"Many contemporary authors drink more than they write."

Maxim Gorky

****

"Many people - and I think I am one of them - are more productive when they've had a little to drink. I find if I drink two or three brandies, I'm far better able to write."

David Ogilvy

****

"My god so much I like to drink scotch that sometimes I think my name is Igor Stra-whisky."

Igor Stravinsky

****

"My idea of working out is drinking whiskey - instead of beer."

Travis Fimmel

****

"My life is ruled by four W's:
my writing, my work, my wife, and my whisky.
Not necessarily in that order."

Ashwin Sanghi

****

"My rule of life prescribed as an absolutely sacred rite, smoking cigars and also the drinking of alcohol before, after and if need be during all meals and in the intervals between them."

Winston Churchill

****

"Never accept a drink from a urologist."

Erma Bombeck

****

"Never delay kissing a pretty girl or opening a bottle of whisky."

Ernest Hemmingway

****

"Ninety percent I'll spend on good times, women and Irish Whiskey.
The other ten percent I'll probably waste."

Tug McGraw

****

"No married man is genuinely happy, if he has to drink worse whisky than he used to drink when he was single."

H. L. Mencken

****

Not all chemicals are bad.
Without such chemicals as Hydrogen and Oxygen, for example, there would be no way to make water, a vital ingredient in whisky."

Dave Barry

****

"Of course, one should not drink much, but often."

Henri de Toulouse-Lautrec

****

"Once during prohibition, I was forced to live for days on nothing but food and water."

W. C. Fields

****

"One does not leave a convivial party before closing time."

Winston Churchill

****

"One drink is too many for me and a thousand not enough."

Brendan Behan

****

"Only Irish coffee provides in a single glass all four essential food groups - alcohol, caffeine, sugar and fat."

George Miller

****

"People are saying that I'm an alcoholic, and that's not true, because I only drink when I work, and I'm a workaholic."

Ron White

****

"People who drink to drown their sorrow should be told that sorrow knows how to swim."

Ann Landers

****

"Sleep - the most beautiful experience in life - except drink."

W. C. Fields

****

"So, let's knock a couple back and make some noise."

Oscar Wilde

****

"Teetotalers lack the sympathy and generosity of men that drink."

W. H. Davies

****

"Tell me what brand of whiskey that Grant drinks. I would like to send a barrel to my other generals."

Abraham Lincoln

****

"The blues is losing someone you love and not having enough money to immerse yourself in drink."

Henry Rollins

****

"The light music of whiskey falling into a glass, an agreeable interlude."

James Joyce

****

"The most important things to do in the world are to get something to eat, something to drink and somebody to love you."

Brendan Behan

****

"The problem with the world, is that everyone is a few drinks behind."

Humphrey Bogart

****

"The transformation of new spirit into mature whisky is as miraculous as the change from Caterpillar to butterfly.
The chrysalis is the Cask."

Dr Jim Swan

****

"The water was not fit to drink. To make it palatable, we had to add whisky.
By diligent effort, I learnt to like it."

Sir Winston Churchill

****

"There are only two real ways to get ahead today - sell liquor or drink it."

W. C. Fields

"There is good whisky, there is whisky that is not so good, but there is no bad whisky."

Dr Philip Schidrowitz

****

"There is no bad whiskey.
There are only some whiskies that aren't as good as others."

Raymond Chandler

****

"There were years when I was a beer and tequila guy, then I got real fat.
And then I found that you could actually go on a diet and drink scotch.
Then I got hooked on scotch, and if you get hooked on scotch, then everything else just tastes wrong."

Ron White

****

"There's nothing wrong with sobriety in moderation."

John Ciardi

****

"They say some of my stars drink whiskey, but I have found that ones who drink milkshakes don't win many ball games."

Casey Stengel

****

"This is Scotland of course not liking whisky is a crime."

Roger Wakefield MacKenzie
("Dragonfly in Amber" by Diana Gabaldon)

****

"Too much of anything is bad, but too much whiskey is barely enough."

Mark Twain

****

"We frequently hear of people dying from too much drinking.
That this happens is a matter of record.
But the blame is always placed on whisky.
Why this should be I never could understand.
You can die from drinking too much of anything - coffee, water, milk, soft drinks and all such stuff as that.
And as long as the presence of death lurks with anyone who goes through the simple act of swallowing. I will make mine whisky."

W.C. Fields

****

"While I can't walk on water,
I can certainly wobble on whisky."

Ashwin Sanghi

****

"Whiskey is liquid sunshine."

George Bernard Shaw

****

"Whisky, like a beautiful woman, demands appreciation."

Haruki Murakami

****

"Whisky should be dark as hell, strong as death, and sweet as love."

J. Hammerstone

****

"Who loves not women, wine and song,
Remains a fool his whole life long."

John Henry Voss

****

"Wild Turkey whiskey and Philip Morris cigarettes are essential to the maintenance of human life!"

Herb Kelleher

****

"Work is the curse of the drinking classes."

Oscar Wilde

****

"Worthless people live only to eat and drink;
people of worth eat and drink only to live."

Socrates

****

"You can't drown yourself in drink.
I've tried, you float."

John Barrymore

****

"You pretty much can't get away from bacon or
whiskey in the South.
Put a doughnut in it and you'd be good to go."

Hillary Scott

****

"You're not drunk if you can lie on the floor without holding on."

Dean Martin

****

Chapter Five

Toasts

Drinking to people's health in:

Afrikaans: Gesondheid (Ge-sund-hate)
Meaning: Health

Albanian: Gëzuar (Geh-zoo-ah)
Meaning: Cheers

Armenian: Կէնաձդ (Genatzt)
Meaning: Life

Bosnian: Živjeli (Zhee-vi-lee)
Meaning: Cheers

Bulgarian: Наздраве (Naz-dra-vey)
Meaning: Cheers

Chamorro (Guam): Biba (Bih-bah)
Meaning: "long live" or "hurray".

Chinese (Mandarin):干杯 / gān bēi (Gan bay)
Meaning: Cheers

Croation: Živjeli / Nazdravlje (Zhee-ve-lee / Naz-dra-vlee)
Meaning: Cheers

Czech: Na zdravi (Naz-drah vi)
Meaning: Cheers

Dutch: Proost (Prohst)
Meaning: Cheers

Estonian: Terviseks (Ter-vih-sex)
Meaning: Cheers

French: Santé! / À votre santé! (Sahn-tay / Ah la votre sahn-tay)
Meaning: To your health

Finnish: Kippis (Kip Piss)
Meaning: Cheers

German: Prost / Zum wohl (Prohst / Tsum vohl)
Meaning: Cheers/ to your health

Greek: Υγεια (Yamas)
Meaning: Health

Hebrew: לחיים (L'chaim)
Meaning: To Life

Hungarian: Egészségedre (Egg-esh ay-ged-reh) or Fenékig (Fehn-eh-keg)
Meaning: (to your health) or (until the bottom of the glass)

Irish Gaelic: Sláinte (Slawn-cha)
Meaning: Health

Italian: Salute / Cin cin (Saw-lutay / Chin chin
Meaning: Health/ cheers

Japanese: 乾杯/ Kanpai (Kan-pie)
Meaning: Cheers/ Empty the glass

Korean: 건배 (Gun bae)
Meaning: Cheers

Lithuanian: Į sveikatą (Ee sweh-kata)
Meaning: To your health

Moldovan: Noroc (No-rock)
Meaning: Luck

Mongolian: Эрүүл мэндийн төлөө (ErUHl mehdiin toloo)
Meaning: For health

Polish: Na zdrowie (Naz-droh-vee-ay)
Meaning: To your health

Portugese: Saúde (Saw-OO-de)
Meaning: Health

Russian: На здоровье (Na zdorovie)
Meaning: To your health

Spanish: Salud (Sah-lud)
Meaning: Health

Swedish: Skål (Skawl)
Meaning: Cheers

Tai: Chok dee (Chok dee)
Meaning: Good luck

Welsh: Iechyd da (Yeh-chid dah)
Meaning: Good health

Yiddish: Sei gesund (Say geh-sund)
Meaning: Be healthy

****

During the Middle Ages, the Vikings were raiding throughout Europe. After winning a battle, Viking warriors would decapitate the king or leader of the tribe/army they had just defeated, and that night would drink from his skull ("Skoll" is a common toast still used in Scandanavia).

****

"Gentlemen start your livers."

****

"Health to those I love, wealth to those who love me."

****

"Here's hoping you live forever
And mine is the last voice you hear."

****

"Here's to a long life and a merry one
A quick death and an easy one
A pretty girl and an honest one
A cold drink—and another one.

****

"Here's to cheating, stealing, and drinking.
May you cheat death, steal hearts,
and always drink with me.

****

"Here's to love, the only fire against
which there is no insurance."

****

"Here's to roses and lilies in bloom, and you in
my arms, and me in your room.
A door that is locked, a key that is lost, a bird
and a bottle and a bed that is tossed.
And a night that is 50 years long."

****

"Here's to steak when you're hungry
Whiskey when you're dry
A lover when you need one
And Heaven when you die."

****

"Here's to the nights we'll never remember
with the friends we'll never forget."

****

"Here's to those who've seen us at our best
and seen us at our worst and cannot tell the
difference."

****

"Here's to whiskey, scotch and rye
Amber, smooth, and clear
Not as sweet as a woman's lips
But a damn sight more sincere."

****

"I drink to myself and another and may that other be he who drinks to himself and another and may that other be me!"

****

In the Elizabethan era, the flavor of wine was improved by dropping a piece of spiced bread into a flagon or cup.
In Shakespeare's "The Merry Wives of Windsor," Falstaff demands, "Go fetch me a quart of sack; and put a toast in't." and we still toast to this day, just without the bread.

****

"May neighbors respect you,
Trouble neglect you,
The angels protect you,
And heaven accept you."

****

"May the best of the past be the worst of the future."

****

"May the hinges of friendship never grow rusty,
nor the wings of love lose a feather!"

****

"May those that love us, love us;
and those that don't love us, may God turn their hearts;
if he can't turn their hearts, then may he turn their
ankles, so we'll know them by their limp."

****

"May we always be happy, and our enemies know it."

****

"May we kiss who we please,
And please who we kiss."

****

"May we live respected and die regretted."

****

"May you always lie, cheat, and steal.
Lie beside the one you love, cheat the devil,
and steal away from bad company."

****

"May you be in Heaven half an hour before
the devil knows you're dead."

****

"May you live for as long as you want,
and never want for as long as you live!"

****

"May our children have wealthy parents."

****

"May you have the hindsight to know where you've
been, the foresight to know where you are going,
And the insight to know when you have gone too far."

****

"My friends are the best friends
Loyal, willing and able.
Now let's get to drinking!
All glasses off the table!"

****

"Oh Whisky! Soul o' plays and pranks!
Accept a bardie's grateful thanks!"

****

"People talk about our drinking
But never about our thirst."

****

"Rejoice and be of good cheer!
For THEY are out there, and WE are in here!"

****

"Success to the lover
Honor to the brave
Health to the sick
And freedom to the slave."

****

The Greeks claim the first written mention of a toast. Odysseus drinks to the health of Achilles during a feast scene in The Iliad.

****

"The wonderful love of a beautiful maid,
and the love of a staunch true man,
and the love of a baby unafraid, have existed since life began.
But the greatest love, the love of love, even greater than that of a mother,
is the tender, passionate, infinite love of one drunken sod for another."

****

"There are good ships,
and there are wood ships,
The ships that sail the sea.
But the best ships, are friendships,
And may they always be."

****

"To the rapturous, wild, and ineffable pleasure
Of drinking at somebody else's expense."

****

"We're only here for a short time, let's make it a good time!"

****

"Wise, kind, gentle, generous, sexy
But enough about me, here's to you."

****

"You're a gentleman and a scholar
and a good judge of bad liquor."

Chapter Six

Facts, Stories & Trivia
(Mostly true, at time of printing)

39 bottles of scotch are shipped every second.

****

60% of the cost of a bottle of Bourbon is tax.

****

80% of the cost of a bottle of Scotch whisky is tax. The spirit must be distilled and matured for a minimum of 3 years in oak casks then bottled in Scotland for it to be called Scotch.

****

A cooper's apprentice must work accompanied for four years before being allowed to tackle their own barrel.

A royal footman who poured whisky into the Queen's corgis' water bowl as a party trick was demoted and had his salary cut.

****

According to legend, the concept of "proof" comes from sailors in the British Royal Navy, who (back in the 18th century) would douse a spoonful of gunpowder in rum as a test of its potency.
If the wet gunpowder still ignited, it was "proof" the alcohol content was high enough, 57% ABV.
If it didn't ignite, well, you probably had some angry sailors on your hands.

****

According to The French Federation of Spirits, whisky accounts for the highest retail sales of any spirit in France at 47.2 per cent.
This is compared to Cognac which makes up only 0.7 per cent of sales.
Put another way, the French drink more Scotch in a month, than Cognac in a year.

****

According to the Kentucky Distillers Association 95 per cent of all bourbon whiskey is produced in Kentucky.
But Bourbon can be made anywhere in the United States, not just Kentucky, in fact, Bourbon is currently being produced in all 50 states.

****

According to the Scottish Whisky Regulations of 2009, Scotland is divided into two protected localities (Campbeltown and Islay (pronounced Isla) and three protected regions (Highland, Lowland, and Speyside).

****

After Prohibition ended, 69-year-old James B. Beam got his distillery up and running in just 120 days.

****

After the introduction of taxes on distilling in Scotland in the 17th century, illicit distillers had to go to great lengths to avoid the taxman.
There are accounts of barrels being hidden in surprising places including beneath broody hens, in funeral corteges and barrels being 'nursed' by breastfeeding mothers.

All Bourbons are whiskey. Always, 100% made in America, 51% corn (Minimum), new charred oak barrels.

How did Bourbon come about?

In 1776, Kentucky County was carved from the massive western part of Virginia previously known as Fincastle County, and a law known colloquially as "Corn patch and cabin rights," was issued by the Virginia General Assembly. The law allowed settlers to lay claim to 400 acres of land provided that they build a cabin and planted a patch of corn prior to 1778.

1792 Kentucky becomes a state.

Meanwhile in nearby Pennsylvania, most of America's favorite drink was being produced and that was Rye whisky, which was being taxed by the federal government, this caused the whisky rebellion.
With 5,000 Pennsylvanians rising in revolt against the tax.
Until George Washington led 13,000 troops into Pennsylvania and quashed the rebellion.

This caused many whisky makers to move from Pennsylvania to the new state of Kentucky.
Where the main crop being grown was corn ("corn patch and cabin rights,"), so they stopped making whiskey with Rye and started using Corn.
So, a lot more Bourbonesque whisky began to be produced, although it wasn't yet called Bourbon.

So, when was Bourbon as we know it, first made?

Estimates say, sometime between 1823 and 1845

Who was the first to make Bourbon, as we would recognize it today?

A likely candidate was Dr. James Crow, a born and bred Scotsman, was working at a distillery in Kentucky around 1823.
Crow was a man of medicine and a man of science, and it was he who experimented scientifically with using setback (sour mash) to control certain aspects of his whiskey-making methods.
His whiskeys, Old Crow and Old Pepper, were very popular during the Civil War, and he has always been hailed as the man who not only made good bourbon, but also knew exactly why his bourbon was good.
He had the scientific knowledge to be able to tinker intelligently with various aspects of his processes in order to make a better whiskey.
He made whiskey using corn as the predominant grain, he insisted on aging it in charred oak casks, and he used a sour-mash starter.
For those who insist on having a name, Dr. James Crow is the "inventor" of bourbon as it is known today, sometime between 1823 and, say, 1845.

****

"America's First Spirit" Laird's Applejack can trace its roots to Scotsman William Laird, most probably a whisky distiller, and originally from Fife, Scotland. Laird settled in Monmouth County, New Jersey, in 1698 and set about applying his knowledge of distillation to apples rather than barley malt. Cider-makers who didn't possess a still would, during the winter months, leave cider outside to freeze.
The following morning, they discarded the frozen portion, leaving them with very strong cider--the alcohol content was concentrated in the liquid that didn't, or couldn't, freeze.
Since the distillation of beverage alcohol is, in simple terms, the separation of alcohol from water, they were performing a form of distillation by freezing instead of heating.

****

An 1896 Scotch from Ernest Shackleton's Antarctic expedition was found in 2006 and is being preserved in New Zealand.
It didn't freeze at -30 temperatures.
In 2011 The Whyte & Mackay company produced a reproduction of this whisky, which in my opinion, is superb.
I currently have a bottle of it on my bar.

****

Andrew Usher, the son of an Edinburgh-based spirits dealer, pioneered Scotch blending in the mid-19th century.

****

Ardbeg (in October 2011) sent a vial of whisky in a cargo spacecraft to the International Space Station to test how zero gravity affects the maturation process. Another vial of the same whisky was kept at the distillery for comparison. The company had set up the experiment to investigate how micro-gravity would affect the behavior of terpenes, the building blocks of flavour for many foods and wines as well as whisky spirits.
Ardbeg commemorated this space experiment by releasing a whisky called "Galileo" in 2012, which if you like smoky whisky is very tasty.

****

At the beginning of the Second World War in 1939, the actor David Niven volunteered to re-join the British Army. He had been in briefly as a younger man. He saw active service in Europe and rose to the rank of Lieutenant Colonel. Understandably concerned for his future, but determined to 'do his bit', he went to see his friend Clark Gable and his wife to say farewell. Gable gave him some wise words of advice for his return to soldiering: 'Stick to Scotch if you want to be brave – gin only makes you piss.'

At the time of writing, there are 128 distilleries licensed to produce Scotch whisky and Scotland is one fifth the size of California.

****

Bailey's Irish Cream – a blend of cream and Irish whiskey – did not come into existence until 1974. It was the first Irish cream to be commercialized.

****

Before they started blending and selling Scotch, the Chivas brothers ran a grocery store in Aberdeen, Scotland.
It opened in 1801, yet the brothers wouldn't start producing whisky until almost half a century later.

****

Blended whisky is responsible for about 90% of all Scotch whisky sales.
A blended whisky is more than just simply a mix of whisky from two different distilleries, blended scotch whisky may contain as many as 40 or 50 different malt and grain (Corn, wheat etc.) whiskies.
The normal ratio of malt to grain is 60% grain 40% malt.

The percentage of malt used will determine the quality, smoothness, taste and character.
Grain whisky is easy and inexpensive to produce, using continuous distillation in large and highly efficient column (Coffey) stills, but the spirit is lighter and has less character.
Malt whisky is expensive and slow to produce but has a more intense flavor.
The Master Blender carefully selects spirit from many different distilleries, skillfully reproducing the character of previous bottlings so the customer enjoys the same taste year after year.
The practice of blending Scotch whiskies started in the mid 1800's.
The original family-run distilleries did not have bottling facilities.
They used to sell whole casks of whisky to bottlers, blenders and merchants who then combined the product of various distilleries, to craft a consistent "brand style."

****

A closed bottle of whiskey, even if it is given as a gift to you on the day you are born, will outlast you even if you live to be one hundred-years-old.
And after you open a bottle of whiskey, a half-full bottle will remain good for five years.
But whisky is for drinking, not to save it for a special day, that day may never come, open it and enjoy it.

Bootlegging a name that came about after smugglers hid their whisky in their boots and legs of their pants.

****

Canadian whisky was once known as 'Brown vodka'.

****

Charles Joughin, the baker on-board the doomed *Titanic*, trod water for three hours before being rescued.
He claimed he hadn't succumbed to the cold due to the amount of whisky he had drunk prior to the accident, while the ship was sinking.

****

Controversial German producer G-Spirits caused quite the stir in 2012, when it said every single one of its products had been poured over the naked breasts of a model prior to bottling.
Its cask strength whisky has been poured over the chest of Playmate Alexa Varga.

****

Crown Royal was first made in 1939, for King George VI and Queen Elizabeth when they became the first reigning monarchs to visit Canada.

Crown Royal was released in the United States in the 1960s and has since become the top selling Canadian whisky.

****

Do you like ice in your Whisky?

Reducing the temperature of the whisky "freezes" the aroma and the taste, and makes your drink taste dull, and flat.......Just sayin'.

****

Drinkers in Scotland tend to drink Scotch with a dash of water.

Drinkers in Spain mix their Scotch with Cola.

Japanese drinkers like a lot of ice and water with their Scotch.

In China the locals like their Scotch with Green Tea!!!!

In France the preference is for ginger ale.

In Brazil it's with sugar cane water.

Drinking one to six glasses of whiskey a week can lower an adult's risk of dementia.
A 2003 case study with the Beth Israel Deaconess Medical Center found that the odds of incident dementia were lower among those adults who consumed moderate alcohol, rather than none at all!

****

During a discussion among the club's membership board at St. Andrews in 1858, on how many holes made a round of golf.
A senior member pointed out that it takes exactly 18 drinks to polish off a fifth of Scotch.
By limiting himself to only one drink of Scotch per hole, he figured a round of Golf was finished when the Scotch ran out.

****

During the Great Fire of Glenrothes in 1922, the casks in storage burst and whisky ran through the streets. With locals frantically trying to save as much of the free whisky as they could.

****

During the malting process, the barley was traditionally turned with a shovel to promote even malting and reduce the tangling of barley sprouts. As a result of this repetitive motion maltsters suffered a condition which caused one arm to hang lower than the other – known as monkey shoulder. In honor of those hard-working men William Grant & Sons brought out a blended malt whisky called "Monkey Shoulder."

****

During World War II, many bourbon distilleries were converted in order to make fuel and penicillin.

****

Early in 2018, the world's first regulated whisky investment fund was launched.
Single Malt Fund allows investors to buy a small part of a bigger collection of rare and limited-edition whiskies.

****

Famous Bourbon drinkers you may know:

US President Martin Van Buren (was known as "Whiskey Blue").

****

US President Zachary Taylor. During the Mexican War, a political aide visited to inform Taylor that the Whig party wished to nominate him for president. Taylor allegedly replied:
"Stop your nonsense and drink your whiskey!"

****

US President and General Ulysses S. Grant. Abraham Lincoln when told that Grant drinks too much whiskey said, "Find out what whiskey Grant drinks and send a barrel of it to my other generals and maybe they will fight."

****

US President Harry S Truman. Truman loved bourbon and quite often knocked down a shot of it in the morning.

****

For many whisky producers, the size and shape of the still is as important a factor as barley, yeast or water to the character of the spirit.
So much so, that when a still is replaced, every dent in the old still is replicated in the new still.

****

Frank Sinatra was buried with a bottle of Jack Daniel's.

****

From the early 1800's up until the 1950's when they died out due to television. Medicine shows travelled across America.
The shows were interspersed with advertising to buy the patented medicine, the main ingredient of the medicines was whisky.
When TV started, just like the medicine shows they had ads/sponsors some of which were whisky

****

Gary "Eggsy" Unwin (the hero) gets offered a 64-year-old Dalmore by the bad guy in the movie "Kingsman: The Secret Service."
How come all the bad guys have great whisky?

****

General George Washington wrote to John Hancock, then president of the Congress.
"The benefits arising from the moderate use of strong Liquor have been experienced in all armies, and are not to be disputed,"

****

George Washington is the only sitting President to lead troops into battle, when he led 13,000 troops into Pennsylvania to crush the "Whiskey Rebellion."

****

George Washington after he retired from office had a commercial distillery at Mount Vernon.
It was one of the biggest distilleries of its time, producing 11,000 gallons of Rye whiskey per year, but was unfortunately destroyed by a fire a few years after opening.
The distillery has been reconstructed and you can tour it at Mount Vernon today.

****

Glengoyne Distillery, a few miles north of Glasgow, is classified as a highland malt whisky as the distillery lies just north of the highland line (an imaginary line that runs from Dundee in the East to Greenock in the West.
But its whisky matures across this line in the lowlands just across the A81 road.

****

Good guys finally win out in the movie "Star Trek Beyond." When Dr McCoy and Captain Kirk share a bottle of Glenfiddich 30-year-old.

****

Glenturret's distillery famous cat, Towser the Mouser, is believed to have caught 28,899 mice in its 24-year lifetime, which begs the question: who was counting?

****

Harrison Ford's character "Deckard" drinks Johnnie Walker Black Label in the movie "Blade Runner."

****

Iceland is home to just two whisky distilleries, both of which use sheep manure in place of coal/peat as a fuel for kilning barley.

****

If bourbon is aged for more than two years but less than four, it must bear an age statement on the label.

In 1922 Chicago doctors prescribed some 200,000 gallons of 'medicinal' spirit.

****

In 1929 six Kentucky distilleries were licensed to produce whiskey for medicinal purposes. Operating as the American Medicinal Liquor Company they proceeded to keep doctors busy by producing 1.4 million gallons of medicinal bourbon per year.

****

In 1930 during prohibition, no fewer than 282,122 stills were discovered in the USA.

****

In 1956, Whiskey replaced William in the NATO phonetic alphabet.

****

In 2009, Tomintoul created the world's largest bottle of single malt Scotch whisky which at 105.3 litres was big enough to fill more than 150 standard-size 70cl bottles.

Brand owner Angus Dundee Distillers donated the 14-year-old liquid to local businessmen Dru McPherson and Mike Drury who created a gigantic cork and an oversized label.

The bottle was officially certified by Guinness World Records as "The Largest Bottle of Scotch Whisky in the World."

****

In 2017 Scottish scientists powered a car using a biofuel derived from whisky residue.

Most whisky residue in Scotland is used for cattle feed.

****

In 2017 a 30-year-old cask of Macallan set a new world record for the most expensive whisky cask ever sold at auction.

It fetched a whopping £375,000.

****

In a study published by the journal *Chem*, researchers used fluorescent dyes to map age, area of origin and taste of drams from the US, Scotland and Ireland.
They hope to harness these findings and develop a method of detecting counterfeit whisky and other alcohol.

****

In certain Latin American countries, people say 'whisky' instead of 'cheese' when posing for photographs.

****

In English pubs, ale was ordered in pints and quarts......So in old England, when customers got unruly, the bartender would yell at them "Mind your Pints and Quarts and settle down."
This is where the phrase "Mind your Ps and Qs" comes from.

****

In June 1875, a bonded warehouse in the Liberties caught fire, and rivers of burning whiskey flowed through the streets of Dublin like lava.
Titled the Great Dublin Whiskey Fire, the disaster resulted in the tragic loss of 13 lives and 1,900 casks of whiskey.

****

In order to finish the screenplay for the *Blue Dahlia*, writer Raymond Chandler drank whisky for eight days while being supervised by six secretaries, a nurse and a doctor.

****

In Victorian times, some Scottish distilleries allowed workers to stop for a dram each time a bell rang.

****

Ireland's Old Bushmills Distillery claims to be the country's oldest legally functioning distillery. Operations on the present site date back to 1276 by some accounts.

****

Irish coffee recipe

Ingredients
16 oz. hot water
2 tsp. light brown sugar
2 oz. Irish whiskey
1 cup. brewed coffee
1/2 cup. heavy cream for topping

Directions
Prior to making your Irish coffee; In a bowl with an electric mixer or by hand, whisk cream until soft peaks form. Cream should be thick but still pourable.

When the cream is ready, fill two mugs with hot water and let them sit for 2 minutes.

Pour out the water and add 1 tsp light brown sugar to each mug.

Pour in the hot coffee, then add your whiskey of choice and stir to dissolve the sugar.

Top coffee with cream by gently pouring over the back of a warm spoon to form a thick layer on top of coffee.

You could substitute the Irish whiskey, with scotch for a Scottish coffee, or a Japanese whisky for a Japanese coffee, a Bourbon for an American coffee etc., you get the idea.

Islay "Feis Isle" Festival - The Islay Festival of Music and Malt
Every year we have a diverse program featuring traditional music, ceilidhs, Gaelic lessons, golf, bowling and whisky tasting.
The Festival is held in the last week of May every year.
For the last number of years all the Islay Distilleries have held open days throughout the week of the festival, adding to the mix!

****

It was the accepted practice in Ancient Babylon 4,000 years ago that for a month after the wedding, the bride's father would supply his new son-in-law with all the mead he could drink. Mead is a honey beer and because their calendar was lunar based, this period was called the honey month, which we know today as the "honeymoon."

****

Jack Daniel learned to distil whisky from a Lutheran minister by the name of Dan Call and an enslaved man named Nathan "Nearest" Green. Jack would later hire Nearest as his head distiller.

****

Jack Daniel's is Tennessee whiskey, not bourbon.

****

James Bond is offered a 50-year-old Macallan by the baddie in the movie "Skyfall." How come all the bad guys have great whisky?

****

Japanese whisky makers rarely trade casks with one another due to how competitive the market is.

****

Joe Sheridan, a head chef in Foynes, County Limerick claims to have invented and named the Irish Coffee. A group of American passengers disembarked from a Pan Am flying boat on a miserable winter evening in the 1940s, so Sheridan added whiskey to their coffee. When they asked if they were being served Brazilian coffee, Sheridan replied, 'No, Irish coffee". The Buena Vista cafe in San Francisco does not claim to have invented the Irish coffee but does claim to have been the first to serve it in America. On a regular day, the Buena Vista serves around 2,000 Irish coffees—up to 2,500 on a busy weekend day.

Johnny Walker "Black Label makes a brief appearance in the Movie "Raiders of the Lost Ark." In the bar fight in Nepal, Harrison Ford hits a bad guy in the head with a bottle of it. A case of a "shot to the head?"

****

John 'Johnnie' Walker was a grocer in Kilmarnock, Scotland in the mid-1800s who specialized in blending tea before he decided to start blending whisky.

****

John Jameson, the founder of Jameson's Irish whisky was Scottish.
The same John Jameson was the great-grandfather of the radio transmission pioneer, Guglielmo Marconi.

****

Just a coincidence, but the spelling of Whisky or Whiskey; Generally speaking, if the country has an 'e' in it, they spell it with an 'e', if no 'e' in the country, then no 'e' in whisky.

America - Whiskey

Australia - Whisky

Canada - Whisky

India - Whisky

Ireland - Whiskey

Japan - Whisky

Scotland - Whisky

****

Kentucky Colonel is the highest title of honour bestowed by the Commonwealth of Kentucky, given in recognition of noteworthy accomplishments and outstanding service to a community, state or the nation.
Not surprisingly, many bourbon industry figures have been honored with it.

****

Kentucky is home to more barrels of maturing bourbon than people.

****

Kikori is a Japanese whisky made from 100 per cent rice.

****

King George the IV's visit to Edinburgh in 1822. He asked for Glenlivet, which at the time was an illegal whisky.
When some was sent down from the highlands, it came with a note saying it had been long in the wood, the first reference to barrel aging.

****

King William IV issues a Royal warrant in 1835 to Brackla distillery, which then became Royal Brackla whisky.

****

Last year World Whisky Day was celebrated in 47 different countries by more than 25,000 people, If you wish to join in this year go to www.worldwhiskyday.com for more information.

****

Legendary frontiersman Davy Crockett is reputed to have drunk a large draught of moonshine in a single gulp on one occasion.
When the power of speech returned to him, he is said to have commented that it had been so hot he wouldn't need to have his food cooked for a month.

****

Licensed Scotch whisky production was banned from 1757 to 1760 due to a poor grain harvest.

****

Many years ago, in England, pub frequenters had a whistle baked into the rim or handle of their ceramic drinking mugs. When they needed a refill, they used the whistle to get some service.
"Wet your whistle" is the phrase inspired by this practice.

Mizuwari - One of the preferred ways of drinking whisky in Japan is Mizuwari, meaning "mixed with water," take a tall glass (like a highball glass) filled with ice Stir with a bar spoon to chill the glass, then pour out any excess water. Add a shot of whisky to the glass. Stir thirteen and a half times clockwise. Top off with water and stir three and a half times clockwise.

****

Mountain Dew was originally meant to be a whisky chaser.

****

No one knows for certain when distilling came to Scotland or Ireland, it is believed to have been introduced by monks from Europe (Christianity arrived in the 5th century).
Grapes (Brandy) were not available in Ireland or Scotland, so they distilled Barley beer and made whisky.

****

No other spirit has been associated with manhood like scotch whisky. Whether it's the hooking punch in the mouth or just the raw and earthy process by which it is brought forth from barley and water, scotch has held a prominent place in the lives of men from kings to authors to titans of industry.

****

No thank you:

The following adulterations were found being added to cheap whisky and exposed by journalists in 1982;

- Acetic acid
- Burnt Sugar
- Glycerin
- Green tea
- Naphtha
- Pineapple
- Prunes
- Sulphuric Acid
- Turpentine
- Varnish

****

Now I don't know if you remember the first time you ever tasted whisky and the tremendous shock to the nervous system that is.
In Scotland this usually happens around the age of four - Billy Connolly.

****

On May 18th 2018, an ultra-rare bottle of 1926 Macallan broke the record for the most
expensive scotch ever sold at auction.
Bonhams Hong Kong auctioned off one of only twelve 750-milliliter bottles of the 60-year-aged whisky in existence for a staggering $1.01 million, handily smashing the previous record of $624,000.

****

One excise officer in the Glenlivet area of Scotland was dismissed during the 1820s for growing barley and selling it to illicit whisky makers.

****

One of the most unusual Scotch whiskies must surely be the blend Hamashkeh, which is a Kosher whisky, produced to the stringent demands of Jewish dietary law.
Hamashkeh is made at the Invergordon Distillery and a Rabbi is present to guarantee that casks used in the maturation have not previously contained sherry.

****

One large oak tree is said to yield enough wood for approximately three 60-gallon casks.

****

One of the first written accounts of American whisky was in 1620, when Virginia farmer George Sloan wrote in a letter, "We have found a waie to make soe good drink of Indian corne I have divers times refused to drink good strong English beare and chose to drinke that."

****

One of the oldest bottles of Scotch whisky, the Old Vatted Glenlivet 1862, was opened in 2017.
Drops of the rare whisky were captured inside 50 Swiss watches, the most expensive of which cost more than £35,000.

****

Pot still whiskey is made by combining both malted and un-malted barley in the mash bill, prior to fermentation, and then distilling in traditional copper pot stills.

****

Prince Charles' favorite whisky is supposedly Laphroaig.

****

Prince Harry was banned from drinking whisky shots while flying his Apache helicopter.
Top brass told the partying Royal to curb his in-flight Glenfiddich habit on the Apache pilot course or risk being dropped.

****

Prohibition (Temperance) timeline in America:

1907 - Georgia and Oklahoma became the first states to adopt statewide prohibition in the USA during the 20th century.

1908 - Mississippi and North Carolina adopted statewide prohibition.

1909 - Tennessee adopted statewide prohibition.

1912 - West Virginia adopted statewide prohibition.

1913 - The 16th Amendment to the U.S. Constitution was ratified.
It legalized the federal income tax. Previously, the tax on alcoholic beverages had provided approximately one-half to two-thirds of the entire federal revenue. By reducing federal dependence on taxes from alcohol, it eliminated a major objection to prohibition.

1914 - Arizona, Colorado, Oregon, Virginia, Washington State and West Virginia adopted statewide prohibition.

1916 - Colorado, Idaho, Iowa, Michigan, Montana, Nebraska, South Dakota, and Washington adopted statewide prohibition.

1917 - It became a federal crime to sell alcohol to members of the U.S. military forces. Indiana, New Hampshire, New Mexico, and Utah adopted statewide prohibition.

1918 - Florida, Nevada, Ohio, Texas, and Wyoming adopted statewide prohibition. Also, this same year the following states ratified the 18th Amendment; Arizona, Delaware, Florida, Georgia, Kentucky, Louisiana, Maryland, Massachusetts, Mississippi, Montana, North Dakota, South Carolina, South Dakota, Texas, Virginia.

1919 to 1933 Prohibition across all of America, during which the sale, manufacture, and transportation of alcohol were banned
(the Eighteenth Amendment to the United States Constitution).

During this time a smuggler called Captain William McCoy smuggled in genuine Scotch whisky, which became known as "The real McCoy."
Real whisky could be had such as "White Horse" and "Laphroaig" were allowed into the country, but only to be prescribed by doctors for medicinal purposes.

****

Queen Victoria, who liked to have a dram of whisky in her tea in the mornings, issues a Royal Warrant to Lochnagar distillery, it then became Royal Lochnagar. One day her devoted Ghillie John Brown who enjoyed more than his fair share of whisky, stumbled and fell over in front of Queen Victoria. Undismayed, the queen announced to the assembled company that she too had felt an earth tremor.

Rachel Barrie was the first female master whisky blender and has paved the way for even more women joining the industry.

****

Rapper Drake (Virginia Black), UFC champion and boxer Conor McGregor (Proper Twelve), Rock band Metallica (Blackened), singer Bob Dylan (Heaven's Door), Country band "Florida Georgia Line" (Old Camp Whiskey), Singer Darius Rucker (Backstage Southern Whiskey), and Movie Director Brett Ratner (The Hilhaven Lodge Whiskey), and even Montgomery Scott, chief engineer on the Starship Enterprise all have their own whiskey brands.

****

Renowned Victorian Illustrator, Tom Browne, drew a picture of a striding man on a menu during lunch with Lord Stevenson, one of Johnnie Walker's directors.
This eventually became the striding man you see on the bottle today.

****

Robert Burns the Scots poet once had the job of exciseman and wrote fondly of whisky in his poetry.

****

Samuel Kier; Using an old whisky still, experimented and discovered an economical way to
produce kerosene.
Kerosene had been known for some time but was not widely produced and was considered to have little economic value.
But at the time whale oil, the principal fuel for lamps in America, was becoming increasingly scarce and expensive.
Kier began selling the kerosene, named "Carbon Oil", to local miners in 1851. He also invented a new lamp to burn his product.
So, Kier and his whiskey still, helped save the whales from extinction.

****

Scotch exports earned £139 every second in 2017 and is sold in over 200 countries around the world.

Scotch that evaporates during maturation is known as the angels' share.

****

Scotch whisky contributes nearly £5 billion a year to the UK economy.

****

Scotch whisky is sold in 180 markets worldwide.

****

Scotch whisky producer Whyte & Mackay discovered one of the most unusual locations for a bar last year (2018) when it opened its own pop-up on top of a crane in Glasgow.
The elaborate marketing stunt was staged to celebrate the whisky firm's 170th anniversary.
The Lion's Clyde bar, which sat in the wheelhouse of the 107-year-old Titan Crane, situated next to the River Clyde, was open for just four days and was thought to be the smallest bar in Scotland.

****

Scotch whisky sells 3 times its nearest rival whisky.

****

The earliest Scottish record of distilling appears in the Royal Exchequer Rolls of 1494, where there is an entry of sale of 'eight bolls of malt approx. 1220kgs (2690 lbs.) of malt to one Friar John Corr 'wherewith to make aqua vitae'.
A boll was an old Scottish measure of between 5 and 6 six bushels. (One bushel is equivalent to 25.4 kgs)

****

Singers Lady Gaga and Pink are reported to prefer Jameson Irish whiskey.

****

Single malt is often mistaken for whisky that only sees one cask.
Really, it's the product of a single distillery so it may actually see multiple casks.

****

Sir Nikola Tesla drank whisky every day because he thought that it would make him live for 150 years. It didn't, but it was worth a shot

****

Some 43 per cent of German tourists in Scotland visit a distillery while visiting, making it the second most popular activity for the demographic.

****

Some distillers are looking beyond traditional grains in the production of whisky. Kentucky-based Corsair produce an expression distilled from red and white quinoa grains.

****

Some people believe bourbon was named after Bourbon County in Kentucky. Others believe it was named after Bourbon Street in New Orleans, a major port for trading Kentucky whisky.

****

Standing at 5.14 meters tall, Glenmorangie's stills are the tallest in Scotland.

****

The ancient Chinese used distilling, as did the ancient Egyptians, but the first recoded use of distilling was the Babylonians (a couple of thousand years BC). Used for the distillation of Perfumes.

****

The average measure of whisky contains just 64 calories – fewer than a banana. Choose wisely!

****

The co-founder of Alcoholics Anonymous, Bill Wilson, demanded whisky on his deathbed but was refused it.

The combination of beer and whiskey is known as a 'boilermaker' in America, where blue-collar laborers regarded it as an effective pick-me-up after a shift down the mines.

****

The famous red-wax sealed Maker's Mark bottle was designed by the distillery owner's wife, Margie Samuels. Samuels wanted something that would stand out in the liquor store and reassure drinkers that this bourbon was quality made. She also came up with the name, which comes from the "mark of the maker," a signature that indicates a product is handmade.

****

The Clydebank area of Scotland was a major target for the German air force during world war II. On the 13th and 14th of March 1941, 200,000 bombs fell on the area badly damaging the distillery.
Since then the Auchentoshan distillery has drawn its cooling water from a giant pond created by a bomb crater.

****

The Diageo Claive Vidiz Scotch Whisky Collection is housed within The Scotch Whisky Experience on the Royal Mile in Edinburgh, Scotland.
This is the World's Largest Collection of Scotch Whisky, with nearly 3,500 individual bottles of whisky housed in this spectacular vault.

****

The first liquor to be made in great quantity in America was, Rum. Around the mid-1600s, Rum was exported from the West Indies to the colonies along with sugar, and molasses from which the colonists made their own Rum.

****

The first Scottish distillery to install a Coffey Still (Continuous still) was the Grange Distillery, which fell silent in 1851.

****

The Glenfiddich bottle is triangular in shape to represent the three pillars of whisky making: air, water and barley.

****

The Guinness World Record for the oldest bottle of whisky in the world belongs to the Glenavon Special Liqueur Whisky.
Bottled between 1851 and 1858, it sold at auction for an astounding £14,850.

****

The Jack Daniel's distillery is in a 'dry county', meaning alcohol sales therein are prohibited. An exception has been made for the distillery.

****

The Japanese have been known to use whisky as an embrocation for cattle, as it is reckoned to make the resultant leather more supple.
The origin of the expression "a drop of the herd stuff?"

****

The "Keeper of the Quaich" is awarded to those who make an outstanding contribution to the Scotch whisky industry for at least five years and outstanding Keepers may progress to become "Masters of the Quaich."

****

The man who drinks scotch is one who lives life to the hilt, savoring new challenges and discoveries on a daily basis.
He doesn't settle and he doesn't drink something just because it's there.
Few men drink scotch to get drunk.
First off, it's too expensive, the cheapest bottles of single malt costing around $40.
But secondly, and much more importantly, each bottle of scotch contains so much history, tradition and attention to detail that the men who drink it are not just downing a beverage but participating in a celebration of artisanship and the deep pleasures of life.

****

The monopoly once in sole charge of producing Finnish alcohol (including whisky) was also responsible for the production of Molotov cocktails for its military.

The only guarantee when talking about whisky, is there will always be someone who disagrees with your opinion of what tastes best and how it should be drunk.

****

The pepper mash in Tabasco sauce is aged in Jack Daniel's barrels before it is then made into the sauce distributed all over the world.

****

The record for most expensive whisky cocktail sold is a refresh of the traditional Manhattan made with a 55-year-old Macallan served at Dubai's Skyview Bar. Costing £4,632, the posh concoction was stirred with a very special oak stick from a cask of Macallan.
It was also served with ice made from the same water used to produce the single malt whisky it contains.

****

The record for the smallest bottle of whisky goes to White Horse, who produced a bottle containing just 1.3 milliliters of whisky.

****

The revolving mechanism that drags heavy copper chains around the base of a still to prevent sticking or scorching is called a rummager.

****

The Royal Brackla Distillery in Nairn, Scotland is situated in the Cawdor Estate, the home of the Thane of Cawdor, Macbeth, in Shakespeare's play.

****

The Scottish Parliament first taxed whisky in 1644.

****

The Scots (and Irish) were distilling "under the shine of the moon", centuries before Moonshiners (mainly descended Scots and Irish) in America.

The SS Politician ran aground with its valuable cargo of 28,000 cases of Scotch whisky off the west coast of Scotland in February 1941.
It was one of the most colorful events in wartime austerity Britain and led to a bestselling novel and an iconic film.
As news of the incident spread, thirsty islanders in small boats began descending on the stricken vessel to help themselves to the precious tipple, which was under strict wartime ration.
What followed was one of the most celebrated episodes of cat and mouse in modern memory as the men of Customs and Excise fought running battles with the islanders to recover the cargo.
The incident inspired the novelist Compton Mackenzie to write his bestselling 1946 novel Whisky Galore - which was adapted into the 1949 film Whisky Galore!

****

The Suntory Yamazaki distillery's first master distiller, Masataka Taketsuru, studied in Scotland before bringing his knowledge home to Japan.

****

The U.S. military is the largest purchaser of Jack Daniels' by the Barrel program.
A service member can purchase an entire barrel of some of Jack Daniel's best whiskey. Various laws and regulations forbid a buyer from taking the 560-pound barrel back to the barracks.
Instead, the spirit is drained off into 250 bottles. So, when U.S. fighters get together to trade war stories, it is often over a glass or two of this historic amber liquid.

****

The writer Albert Mackie considered that the perfect Scottish breakfast consisted of a bottle of whisky, a Haggis and a collie dog.
When asked the purpose of the collie dog, Mackie replied "to eat the Haggis."

****

There are over 300,000 varieties of barley, but only a few are suitable for malt whisky production.

****

There are two things a Highlander likes naked, and one of them is whisky.

****

There is a sign above the door of the Old Fitzgerald Bourbon distillery in Louisville, Kentucky, which reads;
"No chemists allowed. This is a distillery, not a whiskey factory.

****

There were 32,000 speakeasies in New York during prohibition, as opposed to only 15,000 official bars before the Volstead act brought the curtain down on legal drinking.

****

Twenty million casks of whisky are maturing in Scotland currently.

****

US President Dwight D Eisenhower's staff sent a memo to India, before a state visit. "'The President likes Scotch whisky (Chivas Regal, Dimple or Black Dog)."

****

US President Lyndon B. Johnson's favourite brand was Cutty Sark *scotch.* His aide wrote; *'As we drove around his ranch, we were followed by a car and a station wagon with Secret Service agents.*
The President drank Cutty Sark Scotch and soda out of a large white plastic foam cup.
'Periodically, Johnson would slow down and hold his left arm outside the car, shaking the cup and ice.
A Secret Service agent would run up to the car, take the cup and go back to the station wagon.
There another agent would refill it with ice, Scotch and soda as the first agent trotted behind the wagon.
'Then the first agent would run the refilled cup up to LBJ's outstretched and waiting hand, as the President's car moved slowly along.'

****

US President Warren Harding enjoyed drinking whiskey while playing a game of poker with his friends. He also enjoyed drinking whiskey when he played golf (he never shot under 100), we don't know if that was down to the whisky or not.

****

To add Water or not:

This is a personal preference.
Adding water can release the flavors and aromas of the whisky, but something to consider; Tap water may have chlorine in it, and you certainly don't want that in our whisky, so if you add water, use bottled (at room temperature).

****

When Norman Lamont was Chancellor of the UK, in the early 1990s, the bag which was waved at photographers outside No 11 contained a bottle of Highland Park, while the speech itself was carried in a plastic bag by his then-aide, William Hague.

****

When Woodrow Wilson left the White House in 1921 (During prohibition), a cask of Scotch whisky was included in the stock of liquor removed under permit to his new home in Washington DC.

****

While filming in the Congo, most of the cast of *The African Queen* became sick with dysentery from drinking the water.
Director John Huston and actor Humphrey Bogart emerged unscathed, allegedly because they drank nothing but whisky during the shoot.

****

Whiskey is the official state beverage of Alabama.

****

Whisky casks come in various sizes (Good luck, trying to find a standard list) a rough guide is shown below;

Octave
20.5 liters - 5 gallons USA

Pin
20.5 liters - 5 gallons USA

Anker
40 liters - 11 gallons USA

Firkin
40 liters - 11 gallons USA

Blood Tub
50 liters - 13 gallons USA

Quarter cask
1250 liters - 33 gallons USA

Rundlet
68 liters -18 gallons USA

Kilderkin
82 liters - 22 gallons USA

Tierce
159 liters - 42 gallons USA

Barrel
200 liters - 53 gallons

Hogshead
225 - 250 liters - 59 to 66 gallons USA

Barrique
225 - 300 liters - 59 to 79 gallons USA

Butt/Puncheon
476 liters -126 gallons USA

Pipe
650 liters - 172 gallons USA

Gorda
700 liters - 185 gallons USA

Tun
982 liters - 259 gallons USA

****

Whisky in Scots Gaelic reads 'Uisge beathe', which means 'water of life'. English speakers had trouble pronouncing 'Uisge beathe' and abbreviated it to just 'Uisge' which was eventually corrupted to 'Whisky.'

****

Whisky played a key role in westward expansion, approximately one third of the freight being hauled by the railroad in the 1800s was whisky and the revenues from that helped fund the Transpacific railroad.

****

Whisky is low-carb and fat-free, so your thighs will thank you.
One shot has zero fat and .04 carbs.

****

Wild Turkey relies on the same strain of live yeast for a consistent quality across its bourbons.
It therefore makes sense that there's an emergency plan in case anything happens to its Kentucky distillery: the company has secret stashes of its proprietary yeast hidden all across the country.

****

Winston Churchill drank whiskey and soda for breakfast. The whiskey soda washed down his eggs and cigar...well, why not!

****

With a population of 5.3 million, and more than 20 million barrels of whisky in store, Scotland has almost four casks of whisky per citizen.
Laid end to end, these casks would stretch about 30,000 kilometers – or about six times the distance between Edinburgh and New York.
With a value of around £5 billion, Scotch whisky exports accounted for over 20 per cent of all UK food and drink exports in 2017.

****

You can go to college and earn an academic degree in distilling.
Or if you don't want to work in the distilling industry, but want to know more about whisky making, you could do one of the following whisky school programs;

Bruichladdich Academy

Three-day course.

Rough cost: $1,600 per person.

At a seaside distillery on the Isle of Islay that also includes evening trips to the pub,
live folk-music performances, and informal talks on local history.
Face time with the operators in charge of each step of the whisky-making process is a main thrust of the program.

Basic accommodations are provided (for four nights) at the recently refurbished Distillery House.

www.bruichladdich.com

The Jura Fellowship

Four-day course.

Rough cost: $2,000 per person.

One of Scotland's most remote islands (Jura is a two-hour ferry ride from the mainland town of Kennacraig).
Students are housed at the distillery's Jura Lodge, which opened last year and features eclectic interiors—vintage fridges, gazelle antlers, Bakelite phones—by Parisian interior designer Bambi Sloan. The course includes three dinners with tastings and the option of having the distillery age a cask of single malt, that you help bring to the barrel stage.

www.isleofjura.com

****

Middleton Irish Whiskey Academy

Two-day course.

Rough cost: €1199 ($1,350)

The Irish Whiskey Academy at the Middleton Distillery in County Cork, Ireland, offers a two-day Enthusiast Academy, replete with five-star accommodations and a bespoke bottle to take home with your completion certificate.
Follow the whiskey step-by-step from raw materials to maturation, and get hands-on with blending and bottling, all while enjoying several premium tasting sessions.
The Enthusiast Academy is offered twice per year, while a single day Discoverer package is offered monthly for €350 ($400), and a three-hour Academy Experience is offered on an ongoing basis for €95 ($110).

https://www.irishwhiskeyacademy.com

****

Mississippi River Distilling Whiskey School

Length of study: 1.5 days

Rough cost: $2,000 (for two)

Mississippi River Distilling hosts a whiskey school weekend each spring, with the next session scheduled for March 2018.
Learn about the history of whiskey, along with its production and even consumption as you learn to mix classic cocktails.
Tickets are sold in pairs and include overnight accommodations, as well as all food and drink—not to mention six bottles of Cody Road whiskey to help encourage your continued hands-on educational efforts at home.

https://www.mrdistilling.com

****

Spirit of Speyside Whisky School

Length of study: 3 days

Rough cost: £600 ($775)

Held in conjunction with the popular annual Spirit of Speyside festival, this whisky school takes place at the Knockando Distillery and features a diverse lineup of lecturers from across the whisky industry as well as from the Institute of Brewing and Distilling.
Come ready to earn your diploma; with only sixteen slots available for the robust three-day curriculum, this is for serious whisky students.
School is in session from April 30 to May 2, 2018, just prior to the start of the festival, allowing you to enjoy plenty of celebratory drams in the days following graduation.
http://www.spiritofspeyside.com/the_whisky_school

****

Springbank Whisky School

Length of study: 5 days

Rough cost: £1,200 ($1,550)

The production team at Springbank Distillery are your professors for a full five-day school week. Springbank's comprehensive approach includes floor malting and bottling, so you get hands-on with every part of the process.
Pay attention: there will be a test. Following a final session with 50-year industry veteran Frank McHardy, you'll need to pass it to earn your degree—there's no coasting by at Springbank.
Pricing includes nearby accommodations and daily lunch. The school is held weekly from mid-May to the start of July.
http://springbank.scot/whisky-school

I attended the Springbank whisky school in early June of 2016, if you are into whisky and want to visit Scotland, this is ideal. I can't recommend it highly enough, the Springbank school, is off the charts. If I thought that my wife Tracey wouldn't shoot me, I'd go back and do another class!
Here follows my diary from the Springbank whisky school;

Springbank Whisky School Diary

David McDonald and myself (from Northern California, although I was born and raised in Scotland) had decided to indulge our predilection for all things whisky and do a whisky school.

This took place over five days at the Springbank distillery in Campbeltown, on the Kintyre peninsula in Scotland.

My wife Tracey had decided to humor us and amused herself looking around town, while we play (not really, it was hard work) at whisky making. David, Tracey and I stayed at the Ardshiel hotel, about a five-minute walk from the distillery, which by chance has around 750 whiskies in its bar. It's true, if you are good, karma pays you back!

Day one

We arrive at the distillery and meet our fellow class members who are (in no particular order) Roger from Switzerland, Kent from Sweden, Paul from England, Gaetan from Belgium.

All of whom were staying at the recommended B & B "Feorlin", on Longrow, two minutes from the distillery.

We also meet our headmaster for the course Frank McHardy and the distillery manager Gavin McLachlan.

We are given our course book and a very nice Springbank distillery jacket, which under normal circumstances I would have expected to wear during the course, but no, the weather was fantastic for the whole course. We are each allocated a job in the distillery, David and I are sent to the bottling hall, which is semi-automated.

Our first job was to fill the bottles with whisky; David placed 4 bottles and pressed two buttons, pipes came down and filled the exact amount of whisky.

He then passed the bottles to me and I put corks in them, before passing them onto a young lady who held the bottles against a light source to check there were no foreign bodies in the bottle.

She then passed them on to the next stage where a cap was put on the cork. The bottle is now placed on a conveyor which takes it to the first label stop, where the bottle is placed (by hand) into the labeler and a foot pedal is pressed causing a label to be pasted onto the back of the bottle.

When I took my turn at this station, I forgot to take my foot of the pedal and the labels kept on coming, I must have had about a dozen labels stuck on before I realized what I was doing. I had to scrape them off and start again.

The bottle is put back on the conveyor to the next labeling position before being sent along to label quality control and packaging. This was the most fun station as, six of us stood checking the labels and putting the bottles in the boxes, which allowed for many humorous jibes at David and myself (the rookies).

As an unexpected bonus, after work Julie Brown, the Bottling Hall Supervisor gave us each a glass of 18-year-old Springbank to toast my birthday, Karma and timing strike again.

Day two
We start the day Stenciling the whisky's details on the lid of the barrel. Filling barrels (250-liter Hogsheads) with new make spirit, it's not called whisky until it's spent at least three years in an oak barrel.
Then rolling the barrels through the distillery to the warehouse, where they are racked to mature.
The process of racking the barrels is well worth watching, one person climbs up to the relevant shelf and calls down how he wants the barrel to start rolling off the lift onto the rack.
The object is to have the bung at the top of the barrel as it sits in the rack, so there is no spillage, this is achieved by thinking of the barrel as a clock face, with the bung at "noon".
The person on the rack calls down "noon", 12:15, 11:45, 11:30, etc. Whatever starting position, will make the bung finish on the top after it has rolled along the rack, clever stuff.
In the afternoon we observe the grinding of the barley and watch the Mash Tun fill up with the Mash (ground barley and hot water). The mash looks like a huge pot of porridge (oatmeal), and much to my surprise is almost unbearably sweet.

Day three
We start the day on the Malting floor where the barley is drying.
The barley must be turned three times a day to stop the shoots from binding with each other.
The old school way of doing this is to use flat wooden paddles and toss the barley over your shoulder.
We get to turn the barley over, which was hard work in itself, but the next day was a lot harder.

In the afternoon we observed the distillation process.

Day four
There are six tons of wet barley in the "steep" that needs to be taken out and laid evenly on the maltings floor.
This is what hard work feels like.
The barley is shoveled through two manholes in the bottom of the "steep" to the floor below.
We go downstairs and fill wheelbarrows then spread the barley around.

Day five
In the morning we are taken for a walking tour around Campbeltown, our guides Frank and Gavin point out the sites of some of the major distilleries, now gone.
We pay a visit to Glen Scotia and Glen Gyle distilleries and make our way to the Cadenhead tasting rooms on Longrow for a buffet lunch.
In the afternoon we take our exam to see if we've been paying attention.
As we are all whisky geeks the exam is a formality and we are all presented with our certificates and our own individual bottle of Springbank whisky, with our own label on it.

****

Strathearn Distillery Five-Day Whisky School

Length of study: 5 days

Rough cost: £840 ($1,085)

Learning each step of their production process at Strathearn Distillery means being an active part of the team.
Show some ambition and who knows how far you'll go: current distiller and master of wood David Hogg attended the school before landing his gig.
Having helped with everything from mashing to cask filling, you'll have earned your own 2-liter cask of whisky in addition to your certificate.
Shorter three-day (£390/$500) and single-day (£145/$190) programs are also available.

https://www.strathearndistillery.com

All of the above prices are approximate. Visit the distillery school website for current pricing and details.

****

Coppercairn

Not a whisky school per say, but a one of a kind truly unique all-inclusive Scotch whisky experience where you can enjoy insider distillery visits, whisky dinners and tutored tastings all personally hosted by your own professional whisky guide.
Based in the heart of Speyside and offering bespoke experiences, whisky tastings and adventures in Scotland.

www.coppercairn.com

Bibliography

(With thanks to)

Bartending.com
https://barsandbartending.com

****

Brainy Quotes
https://www.brainyquote.com

****

CNN
www.cnn.com

****

Complete Speaker's and Toastmaster's Library
by
Jacob M. Braude

Facebook
https://www.facebook.com

****

Islay "Feis Isle" festival
http://www.islayfestival.com

****

Matador Network
https://matadornetwork.com

****

The Art of Manliness
www.artofmanliness.com

****

The Atlantic
https://www.magazine-agent.com-sub.info/The-Atlantic/Welcome

****

The British Royal Navy
For taking me drinking all over the world
https://www.royalnavy.mod.uk

****

The Guinness book of Poisonous Quotes
by
Colin Jarman

****

The Spirits Business
www.thespiritsbusiness.com

****

The whiskey Wash
https://thewhiskeywash.com

****

Three Sheets to The Wind: Words for Drunk & Hung-over
by Joshua Malin
http://vinepair.com

Today Translations
www.todaytranslations.com

****

Twitter
https://twitter.com

****

Vinepair
http://vinepair.com

****

Whisky a very peculiar History
by
Fiona Macdonald

****

Whisky.com
www.whisky.com

****

Whisky, Wit & Wisdom
by
Gavin D. Smith

****

World Whisky day website
www.worldwhiskyday.com

Biography

Paul Bissett was born in Edinburgh, Scotland and raised in the village of Blackness on the river Forth. At the age of seventeen he embarked upon a twenty-three-year career in the British Royal Navy, which took him all over the world. He has lived and worked in seven different countries.

He has, at various times been; a mountain guide; made and installed kilns in Australia; an instructor in Saudi Arabia; a Documentation Manager for a software company in Taiwan; and in the USA been a salesman for Sears, a firefighter, an Emergency Medical Technician (EMT), a jewelry store manager, Senior Case Manager for the National Expert Witness Network based in Paradise, California and is currently employed by International Network in Advance-Gaming Inc. (INAG).

Outside of work, he conducts Celtic and Scottish weddings. Hosts whiskey tastings, in California, Nevada and Oregon. For fun, he researches all things whisky, and writes/edits a whisky newsletter that go out to readers in ten different countries, with over 250 written so far.
He also gives talks on all things Scottish and has been the Master of Ceremonies at many events all over the world, including the Las Vegas Celtic Games (twice).

He currently lives in Yuba City, California, with his wife Tracey and their three dogs, Heather, Hamish and Luna.

Also, by Paul Bissett;

Children's books

Winter's Bite – (Book one in the series). A modern-day adventure set in Scotland based on Scottish mythology.

Destiny's Bite - (Book two in the series). A modern-day adventure set in Scotland based on Scottish mythology.

Cigars

Cigar Traveler - A guide to Cigar lounges in USA.

Travel Books

From Milngavie to Midges - Hiking the "West Highland Way, Scotland."

Hiking with Nessie - Hiking the "Great Glen Way, Scotland."

Touring Central Scotland – Edinburgh, Falkirk, Glasgow, Stirling etc.

Touring Orkney, Shetland & the North Western Highlands - Including the North Coast 500.

Touring Scotland - A guide to help you plan the trip of a lifetime.

Touring Southern Scotland - Galashiels, Selkirk, Melrose, Hawick, Kelso, Jedburgh & Ayr, Dumfries etc.

Touring the North East of Scotland - Aberdeen, Dundee, Perth, Royal Deeside, Speyside etc.

Touring the West Coast and the Western Isles of Scotland – Campbeltown, Fort William, Islay, Jura, Mallaig, Oban & Skye.

Whisk(e)y Books

A Whisky Might Not Fix Things, But It's Worth A Shot! - Whisk(e)y related: Anecdotes, Humor, Jokes, Memes, Quotes, Toasts & Trivia.

Scotland's Single Malt Whisky Distilleries. Where they are, when they were founded, how to pronounce their names (and what those names mean). I have also included a review of a whisky from each distillery.

Whisky Timeline - Whisk(e)y distilleries around the world and when they were founded.

Whiskey Traveler - A guide to Whisk(e)y bars around the world.

Whiskey Traveler America – Whiskey bars in every state.

Whiskey Traveler Great Britain - Whisky bars in England, Northern Ireland, Republic of Ireland, Scotland & Wales.

Available on: www.amazon.com.

My email is: paulwbissett@outlook.com

My website is: www.scot-talks.com

Made in the USA
Monee, IL
27 April 2022